Month of Mary ~ Queen of France

By Fr. Marin de Boylesve, S.J.

Translated and annotated
by E.A. Bucchianeri

Month of Mary ~ Queen of France

By Fr. Marin de Boylesve, S.J.

Translated and annotated
by E.A. Bucchianeri

Batalha Publishers
Fatima, Portugal

This new English edition has been translated and annotated by E.A. Bucchianeri © 2023 from the Second French Edition published by René Haton, Paris. (1884)

ISBN: 978-989-53726-3-8

Table of Contents

About this Edition **12**

About the Author **13**

Forward by Fr. Marin de Boylesve **25**

ಶಿ⚜ಜ

1 ~ Honour Given to Mary **27**

    ~ Notre Dame de Chartres 29

2 ~ The Greatness of Mary **35**

    ~ The Veil of Mary 38

3 ~ Devotion to Mary **43**

    ~ Imitation 43

    ~ The Kings and Notre Dame de
        Chartres 44

4 ~ Veneration **48**

    ~ The Protestants and
        Our Lady of Chartres 51

5 ~ Invocation 55

~ Notre Dame de Chartres
     after Louis XIII 57

6 ~ The Armour of Mary 60

~ Mary in Paris 61

7 ~ The Weapons of Mary 66

~ The Kings and the Doctors 69

8 ~ The Chaplet or Rosary 77

~ The Protestants and
     the Blessed Virgin of Paris 79

9 ~ Mary in the Divine Plan 82

~ St. Ignatius ~ St Francis de Sales ... 85

10 ~ The Terrestrial Paradise 88

~ The Vow of Louis XIII 90

11 ~ The Tree of Life 94

~ The Miraculous Medal 96

12 ~ Noah's Ark **100**

~ Notre Dame des Victoires 102

13 ~ The Rainbow **105**

~ Mary at Marseilles 107

14 ~ Jacob's Ladder **109**

~ Notre-Dame de Pignans
(Diocese of Fréjus) 109

~Notre-Dame de Grâce at Cotignac
(Diocese of Fréjus) ... 110

~Notre-Dame d'Embrun
(Diocese of Gap) 111

~ Notre-Dame du Laus
(Diocese of Gap) 112

15 ~ The Basket of Moses **115**

~ Notre Dame des Doms (Avignon) 117

16 ~ The Burning Bush **121**

~ Notre Dame de Peyragude
(Diocese of Agen) 123

17 ~ The Rod of Moses **127**

~ Notre Dame du Puy 129

18 ~ The Pillar of Cloud **135**

~ Notre Dame de Grâce (Cambrai) 137

19 ~ The Rock of Horeb **145**

~ Notre Dame d'Avesnières 145

20 ~ Mount Sinai **149**

~ Mary in Anjou 152

~ L'Angevine 152

21~ The Ark of the Covenant **157**

~ The Cathedral of Angers 158

~ Notre Dame du Ronceray 159

22 ~ The Law, the Manna, the Rod **163**

~ Notre Dame du Verger
      or du Rocher 165

23 ~ The Ark, Counsel of Israel 166

~ Notre Dame de Sous-Terre 168

24 ~ The Ark in the Time of Combat 170

~ Notre Dame de Fontevrault 172

~ Notre Dame des Ardilliers 173

25 ~ The Ark among the Philistines 175

~Notre dame de Cunault 177

26 ~ The Ark, the Bethsamites and Oza ...178

~ Le Puy-Notre-Dame 179

27 ~ The Ark and its Blessings 181

~ The Belt of the Blessed Virgin
                    at Loches 181

28 ~ The Ark in the Temple 185

~ Notre Dame de Pontron 185

~ Notre Dame de Béhuart 186

~ Notre Dame de Marillais 186

29 ~ The Interior Life of Mary **188**

~ Notre Dame à la Flèche 191

30 ~ The Virtues of Mary **192**

~ Louis XIII and the
    Immaculate Conception 195

31 ~ Continuation of the Virtues of Mary 197

~ Letter of Louis XIV on the Subject
    of the Immaculate Conception ... 200

ಸಿ ❀ ಜ

APPENDIXES

Appendix One : The Brown Scapular of Our Lady of Mount Carmel

~ A Brief History of the Carmelites 204
~ St. Simon Stock and the
    Revelation of the Scapular 206
~ The Addition of the Sabbatine Privilege 207
~ Questions and Answers
    about the Brown Scapular 208
~ The Investiture Ceremony
    (In Latin and English) 216

Appendix Two: The Blue Scapular of the Immaculate Conception

~ The Story of the Scapular 220
~ Responsibilities of Those
　　Wearing the Blue Scapular
　　and Belonging to the Confraternity 222
~ The Confraternity: Its Aims
　　and Spiritual Benefits 223
~ Feast Days and Indulgences 226
~ Order of Admission and
　　Investiture Ceremony 228
~ Additional Explanations,
　　other Obligations and Privileges 237

Appendix Three: The Red Scapular of the Passion

~ The Story of the Scapular 239
~ The Design of the Scapular 241
~ Obligations of the Red Scapular
　　Confraternity Members 241
~ Indulgences Granted by Bl. Pius IX to the
　　Red Scapular Confraternity Members 242
~ Investiture Ceremony 243

Appendix Four: The Chaplet of the Ten Evangelical Virtues of the Blessed Virgin Mary ... 246

Illustration Credits 250

About this Edition

This new English edition has been translated from the Second French Edition published by René Haton, Paris. (1884). British spelling has been used. This edition features new additions: biography of the author, the footnotes, the appendixes and the illustrations.

E.A. Bucchianeri

About the Author

Fr. Marin de Boylesve was born on November 28, 1813 at the Château de la Coltrie in the commune of Saint-Lambert de la Potherie near Angers. He came from a distinguished aristocratic family whose name can be traced back many centuries as seen in Abbé Jean-Baptiste Ladvocat's *Dictionnaire historique portatif* (1755). Fr. Marin descended directly from Eslienne Boyliaue (or Boilyeve), the great statesman and the principal adviser of St. Louis IX, King of France. Other illustrious ancestors included intrepid knights, one in particular also named Marin joined the cause of King Henry IV. After the Battle of Arques, the king called him 'his beloved knight', granted him a heredity knighthood in 1597, then was made Seigneur de la Maurouziere in 1598 thereby granting him the right to add three gold fleur-de-lis to the top of his arms and bear the signs of the Order of St. Michel in his escutcheon. He was also appointed lieutenant-general of Anjou and councillor of state as a reward for his dedication. Another Marin Boylesve appears in the family line, the third to hold the name, and was in service to King Louis XIV as manager of his hôtel.

Loyal to the French King and to their Catholic faith, many members of the family were forced to emigrate during the French Revolution, but some members stayed behind in their beloved France. Fr. de Boylesve would recall a favourite family story, of how his grandmother was imprisoned in Angers by the Revolutionaries and managed a daring escape on the road during a prisoner transfer to the local castle. While she pretended to pick up a dropped package, a solider kicked her into the ditch. She took the opportunity to flee to a nearby house. However, when they threatened to imprison those harbouring escaped prisoners, she bravely marched straight in to the Revolutionary Office and gave herself up to ensure the safety of those who sheltered her. The revolutionaries did not dare risk upsetting the populace as her father was the former mayor of Angers before the Revolution and loved by the people. They decided to let her return to her father's house.

  Fr. de Boylesve was the last direct descendant of his distinguished line, having followed the call to enter the Company of Jesus, or Jesuits, which also is a remarkable story of a predestined vocation. The Jesuits were persecuted due to fears they were growing in power and wealth. Pressured by the royal courts of Europe, Pope Clement XIV suppressed the Society, forcing members of the order to renounce their vows and go into exile. They were expelled from France in 1764. Fr. de Boylesve's mother, Clémentine de Livonnière, made a solemn promise on the day of her wedding that if God permitted the Jesuits to return to France and she was granted a son, she would offer him to the order and entrust him to it. As mentioned, Fr. Marin was born in 1813, a year before 1814 when Pope Pius VII restored the Society. Tragedy struck when Marin's father died, Marin was only ten months old at the time, but keeping her promise his mother dutifully sent him for his education at the age of ten to the Jesuit Fathers of Montmorillon. The moment he arrived at the school and saw a Jesuit for the first time who happened to be the Superior of the college Fr. Michel Le Blanc, he heard an inner voice say to him: "Little one, that is what you will be."

Fr. de Boylesve entered the school as a student and was destined never to leave the Jesuits. In 1831 he turned eighteen, a year after the July Revolution of 1830, which saw the rightful king to the French throne Charles X overthrown. His heir, Henry V the 'Miracle Child', was forced into exile at the age of ten, his throne usurped by the man who had been approached to be his regent, Louis-Philippe, Duke of Orléans. The events of the times burned the hearts of the faithful as the historical church of the royal family, Saint-Germain-l'Auxerrois, was profaned. Paris was sacked, and wayside devotional crosses and shrines over large areas of France were destroyed as Catholic legitimist symbols of Charles X, even those which had no royal significance or connection to the king.

Fr. Marin had just completed his schooling when he formally announced his decision to enter the Society, the historic events of the previous year and their aftermath no doubt influencing his decision. Writing to his grandmother he declared:

"The course of my studies completed I could not remain without doing anything. God will ask us for an exact account of all the moments He gives us. Full of this thought I ardently wished to serve my country and the Church especially. At a time when both are in such great peril, as a Frenchman and as a Christian, I felt the need to throw myself into the thick of the fray. To take place in the first rows under the banners of religion whose triumph alone can bring glory and happiness back to my homeland, to serve immediately under my first head Jesus Christ, to be one of His companions, seemed to me the most glorious at the same time as most useful for my neighbour. Immense advantages, treasures of happiness and glory, the hundredfold from this life of all that I would give to the Lord, all of these promised in the gospel by Jesus Christ, strongly attracted me to be generous. What more could I do than give myself? (...)"

His family strongly opposed, especially as he was the last direct heir to the Boylesve house, but his mother let him go despite the great sacrifice, no doubt she understood God was accepting her promise to give him to the Jesuits, and not just for his education but now was asking for his whole life, a bitter dreg for her down to the last drop of the cup.

He entered the Novitiate in 1831 at Estavayer in the canton of Fribourg in Switzerland with two other students. As they arrived at their new school, they rang the doorbell at the moment the house clock struck three. The Father who received them remarked: "You are entering at the hour of the Sacred Heart." This introduction to a new school would once again give Fr. de Boylesve a sign regarding the future work he would one day accomplish, although on this occasion he did not know it at the time. He made his first vows at the Maison du Passage on October 10, 1833. He studied philosophy and then in 1835 became a supervisor at the Collège de Mélan, a position he held for one year. He remained in the same college until 1842 where he was in succession professor of grammar, humanities and rhetoric. He thoroughly enjoyed his work with the students, writing in 1837:

"I find this job a lot of fun, despite the hardships that come with it. I have forty students; I love them and I try to spare nothing to make them good Christians, educated Christians capable of one day rendering true service to religion and to the state. It is the sight of such a noble ending that sustains and animates me." In the same letter he continues, regarding his concern for his family, "(...) what the only important thing is, is everyone behaving well and does he remember the motto of the family, RELIGIO, PATRIA? For me who gave up everything, even my name which will be extinguished in my person, I remember it, and God grant that I am consumed and that I use myself in the service of one and of the other."

Although renouncing his aristocratic life he never gave up its noble spirit represented by the family motto, an ardent loyalty to the Catholic faith of his forefathers and his country. In the title pages of his texts he included the family crest of three crosses and motto: RELIGIO, PATRIE – "Faith and Country". Those who knew him and his 'military' style ways said he was just like the loyal intrepid knights of old.

At the end of 1842 he returned to France. He took theology courses at Laval for four years. Instinctively he was drawn to the writings of St. Thomas Aquinas and steered clear of new systems that deviated from the philosophical teachings of the Seraphic Doctor. In 1846 theology training completed, Fr. Boylesve was sent by his superiors to Angers, then in his third year at Notre-Dame d'Ay. In 1848 he was appointed to Brugelette, where he occupied the chair of philosophy. One student who fondly recalled Fr. de Boylesve and his time at Brugelette said his arrival was providential. His classes were easy to follow, his manner clear and crisp, but this is not all that gained the respect of the students. In 1848 they were restless as revolution was in the air, Louis-Philippe I, who had overthrown Catholic King Charles X was now in his own turn overthrown. Rising above and beyond what was required of his philosophy courses, Fr. Boylesve seized the opportunity like a knight-commander of old to direct the lazy students yet bursting with energy towards something constructive: Catholic action to fashion them into vigorous young men of service for Church and country. With his apostolic action he captivated the students with his literature classes, speaking on many subjects from philosophy, history, politics both ancient and modern. He particularly drew them with his catechism lessons on the Council of Trent, his clarity and enthusiasm captivating them.

As Fr. de Boylesve loved his students he was equally admired and loved by them, earning the nickname 'The Captain' as a mark of respect. The students composed a military style tune for his birthday, the refrain remaining popular and hummed everywhere: "Courageous Captain, lead us into battle." A student recalls: "I understood all that was apostolic about his action on us. We can sum it up by saying that he made it his mission to preach to us always and everywhere the contemplation of Saint Ignatius on the Reign of Jesus Christ as it is given in the *Exercises*." In 1851 Fr. Boylesve was sent to Vannes where he was made prefect of studies, his nickname 'The Captain' following him. In October 1853 he left the post and resumed teaching philosophy, a position that he would keep for a long time, either in Poitiers or in Vaugirard.

Known to be quiet and reserved when on his own, it was another matter when he was teaching or publicly speaking. He was incapable of remaining silent or softening his direct manner of expression when it was a question of truth, and did not hold back when it came to defend the Faith and the Church against unbelievers, becoming as noted like his knight-ancestor of old, charging forth to give chase and defeat any bold rascal on the field of battle albeit with his tongue and writings rather than with a literal sword. His attitude is quaintly summed up by the art critique he once gave of the statue of the fountain of St. Michael in Paris, complaining with slight annoyance that the mighty archangel was made to look too carefree and benevolent when dispatching Satan: "See then, it is that he seems to spare him!"

He was also a zealous worker and relished activity. He once wrote: "I challenge my superiors to give me too much work." In addition to his religious duties and teaching, he was a prolific writer, his output seeming to have no end. He wrote on a myriad of subjects and in different genres, from devotional booklets and pamphlets to history, literature, philosophy, Biblical dramas, summaries of the Church Fathers and Doctors, his own sermons, studies of the Scriptures, Our Lady, the *Exercises* of St. Ignatius just to name a few, there were always more plans for further works in progress, his room filled with notes and notebooks. He was always studying as well, also making it a practise to read through the entire Bible every year. One might call him a workaholic in today's terms, but it was noted he believed in a time and a place for everything and diligently managed his hours. He enjoyed recreation time, especially going for walks, and did not sacrifice rest. Despite his zest for work, he disapproved of a few young professors who sacrificed too much sleep and recreation time for their studies, endangering their health. Yet, while sparing of his time, he was ever charitable and ready to help another all for the glory of God.

In September 1870 Fr. de Boylesve was sent to the College of Le Mans, Notre-Dame de Sainte-Croix, when the Franco-Prussian war was raging and France suffered the indignity of invasion. The humiliation felt by the country also struck the pious and patriotic Fr. de Boylesve to the core: "I searched through the memories of my life; I do not remember ever having felt greater pain than this, not even when I learned of my mother's death. This humiliation of France, the Eldest Daughter of the Church, thus succumbing before Prussia, the Eldest Daughter of Protestantism, in the face of the whole world, is something unheard of."

The Messenger, the magazine of the Apostleship of Prayer run by the Jesuits, began spreading the visions of St. Margaret Mary, declaring the only way France would be saved from her enemies was to embrace the devotion to the Sacred Heart. The message inspired Fr. de Boylesve. He became a chaplain to the Catholic Papal Zouaves, forces sent to defend the French Motherland from the Protestant invaders, giving them rousing sermons: "Clotilde, inspiring faith in Clovis, saved the Franks and slaughtered the Germans at their feet ... Joan of Arc by her standard delivered France from the English! Your standard is the Sacred Heart." The Zouaves placed the Sacred Heart on their banner. Fr. de Boylesve also busily spread Sacred Heart badges of wool for the soldiers to pin on their uniforms, for they were in high demand. A gifted and inspiring preacher, his sermons encouraged them onward, even when they were driven back in defeat by the Prussians to where the soldiers remarked: "This man can lead us to the fire tomorrow; we would gladly be killed for him."

Fr. de Boylesve is fondly remembered today in Catholic circles in France for his work as the director of the Apostleship of Prayer in Le Mans through which he contributed to the spread of devotion to the Sacred Heart. On October 17, 1870 Fr de Boylesve was appointed to preach at the Visitation of Le Mans upon St. Margaret Mary for his subject, who at the time was a Blessed. He also preached upon another mystic who had died within their own times, Mother Marie de Jesus (1797-1854) from the convent des Oiseaux of Paris who had received revelations from the Sacred Heart that were favourably recognised by the Archbishop of Paris. On June 21, 1823 the Sacred Heart revealed to Sr. Marie of Jesus that He desired France be consecrated to His Sacred Heart by the King, and that a chapel be built and dedicated to Him, and the feast of the national consecration be formally celebrated every year. "After my sermon," recounts Fr. Boylesve, "the Mother Superior expressed to me her astonishment at my silence with regard to an almost similar order that Our Lord had given to Blessed Margaret Mary on June 17th, 1689. I confessed that in our college, which had barely opened for a month, I had not found the letters of the Blessed One and that I was unaware of the apparition and the order she was telling me about. I promised to make good this omission." Apparently at that time, the Sacred Heart's requests to St. Margaret Mary for a shrine and the national consecration of France by the King were not yet widely known.

True to his word, filled with his characteristic zeal for faith and country, doing what he could to extend the reign of Jesus Christ through his beloved homeland and secure its safety, the very next day he repaired his omission by publishing a pamphlet featuring the prophecies of St. Margaret Mary and Mother Marie de Jesus entitled "Triumph of France by the Sacred Heart", composing a special prayer of consecration, which the Zouaves said every Friday as hope in the Sacred Heart was sorely needed. Paris was threatened with destruction by bombardments, then starvation by the invading Prussians, having commenced a siege around the city in September 1870. The siege continued until January 1871, the citizens reduced to dire circumstances. The zoo animals were slaughtered for food, the populace also living off of stray animals and rats. While the Prussian advance had ceased, humiliation still ensued when France suffered defeat at the hands of the Prussians with the establishment of the German Empire, also losing the territory of the Alsace-Lorraine to the victors. The troubles were not over. From March to May 1871 Paris fell into the clutches of the anticlerical socialist Communards, rebels revolting against the new government of the Third Republic. Blood ran in the streets, historical buildings burned, including the Tuileries Palace. The anticlerical Communards also executed the Archbishop of Paris, Georges Darboy, fulfilling the prophecy of St. Catherine Laboure. This horrific turn of events, combined with the circulation of prophecies foretelling the destruction of Paris was at hand, the faithful no doubt felt doom hung over the city. The times were desperate. After several reprintings, including a full reproduction of the text by Fr. Ramiere in the 'Messenger' newsletter issued by the Apostleship of Prayer, more than 330,000 copies of Fr. de Boylesve's pamphlets of the 'Triumph of the Sacred Heart' were circulated. It contributed to the rapid spread devotion to the Sacred Heart and bolstered the call to have the Universal Church consecrated to the Sacred Heart, also to build a national shrine on Montmartre in atonement for the atrocities committed by the Communards who began their uprising there. Construction began in 1875, the cornerstone was laid on June 16, 1875, the day Bl. Pius IX encouraged all the faithful to pray the consecration to the Sacred Heart using the special formula composed by the Sacred

Congregation of Rites for the 200th anniversary of the apparition of the Sacred Heart to St. Margaret Mary. The construction of Sacre Coeur was at last completed in 1914.

As for Fr. Boylesve, in addition to his efforts to spread devotion to the Sacred Heart he worked unceasingly at many other endeavours, not only as director of the Apostolate of Prayer in Le Mans, but also with the Confraternities of Saint Joseph such as that of the Good Death, and also the Confraternity of the Agonizing Heart, the Work of Campaigns, Conferences of St. Vincent de Paul, Workers' Circles, he still appeared to dare all and sundry that they would never be able to find enough work for him to do. He amazed all that he was never at a loss for a subject to preach upon. He could easily vary his sermons to where it appeared he never preached the same way twice, and always captured his hearers' attention. One day out of curiosity a hardened sinner walked in to listen to him preach and left a converted man.

When Fr. Boylesve was not working, he was praying. There was no question that he maintained a deep spiritual life. He was transferred to Vaugirard in 1875, returning to Le Mans two years later in 1877. Three years later his teaching came to an end at the college there with the decree of March 29, 1880 issued by the French minister for public education prohibiting the Jesuits from engaging in their educational apostolate, only the first of several anticlerical laws that would be passed in France over the next decades. Fr. Boylesve admitted he was on the verge of tears saying his last Mass for the students in the chapel before the school closed. Yet, he remained as active as ever despite this terrible blow, preaching, giving catechisms and continuing his writing, tackling the problems of the day threatening both the Church and society.

He continued working despite his old age, until the end of 1891 when his activity was curtailed. He was struck with various ailments, first a tormenting dermatitis that remained with him, then inflammation of the blood that restricted his activities for many weeks, although he managed to say Mass and continue his writing, until at last he was struck with paralysis, unable to walk or speak. Clutching his rosary and his crucifix, the ever zealous 'priest-knight' of the Vendée gave up his soul to God in February 22, 1892 and was buried in the Jesuit cemetery of Sainte-Croix.[1]

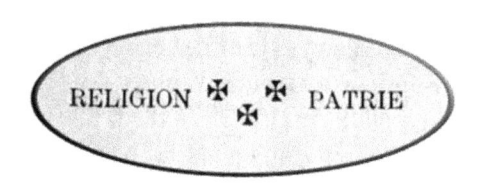

RELIGION ✠ ✠ ✠ PATRIE

---

[1] Biographical information from 'Necrologie. Le Père Marin de Boylesve, in 'Lettres de Jersey', Vol.XII, No. 1 (April 1893)

Forward by Fr. Marin de Boylesve

This "Month of Mary", part of which has already appeared several times, is like the preamble to the one we have published under the title: "The Blessed Virgin According to the Gospels"

The present edition *is more than doubled* by the addition of historical features which intersect the readings on the greatness and veneration of Mary, and on the figures who heralded her in the Old Testament.

These features, except for a few whose sources will be indicated in their place, are taken from or summarized from the great work of Mr. Hamon on "*Notre-Dame de France*".

These facts, which it will be easy to multiply, suffice to justify our title: "Mary Queen of France".

REGNUM GALLIAE, REGNUM MARIAE,
NUNQUAM PERIBIT

Kingdom of France, Kingdom of Mary
Will Never Perish

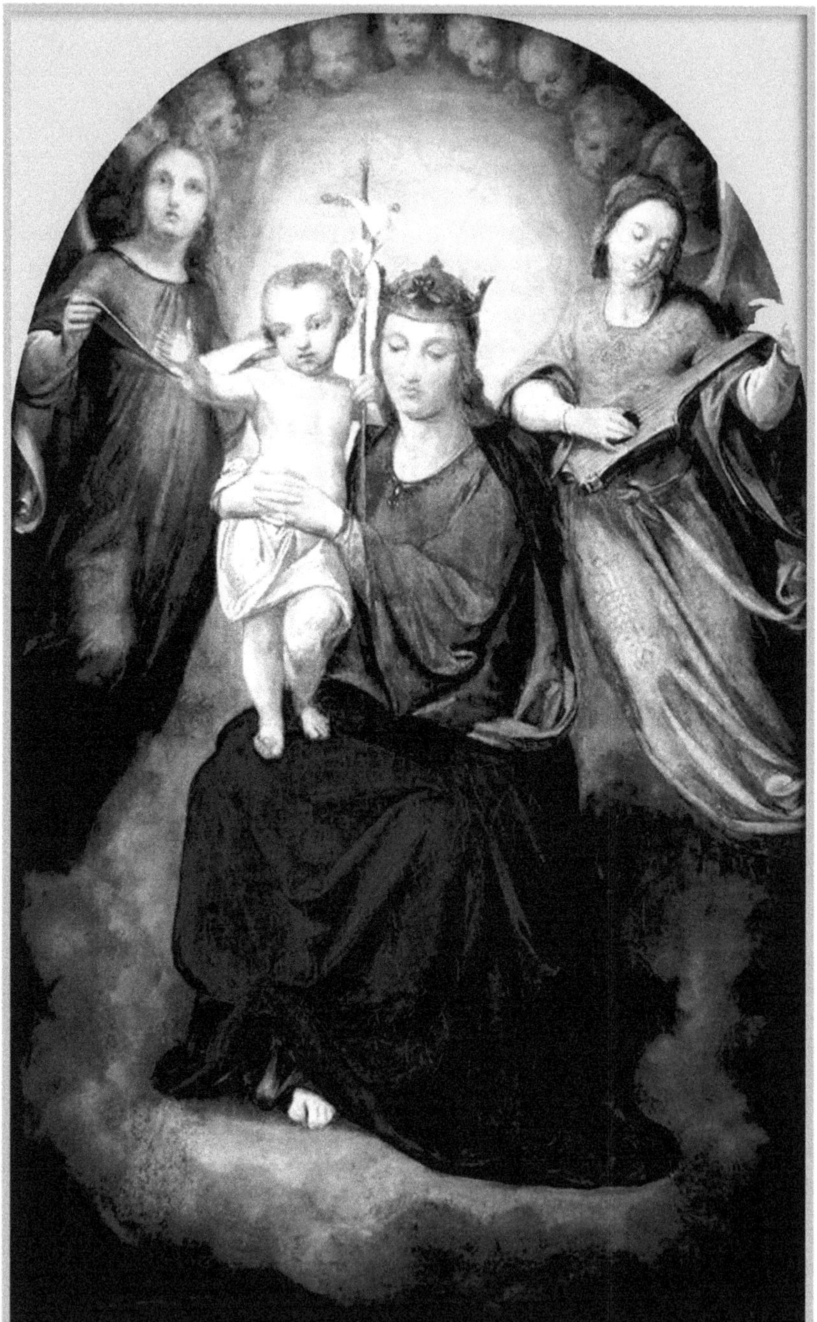

MONTH OF MARY – QUEEN OF FRANCE

1 ~ Honour Given to Mary

God alone has a right to our worship; for He alone is Great, He alone is the Most High, He alone is the Creator, He alone is the Sovereign Saviour. Now, adoration is the act by which we recognize excellence and supreme majesty, authority and sovereign domination.

Between God and man there is only one Mediator, the God-Man, Jesus Christ, in Whom and by Whom we must be saved.

However, God likes to cast a reflection of His greatness on His works; and often to act on the exterior, the Creator is pleased to employ His creatures.

In turn, the Mediator and the only Saviour exercises His mediation and distributes the means of salvation, which are His doctrine and His grace, through the ministry of certain chosen men: such were the Apostles. Today their place is held by the Pope and by the Bishops assisted by the priests.

You honour God, you love Him: honour Him, love Him in those whom He honours and loves; honour Him, love Him in those who represent His power and His goodness. The contempt shown towards envoys sent by a prince and his friends would reflect on his very person. So Jesus Christ says to those whom He sends: "Whoever listens to you, listens to Me; he who despises you, despises Me; whoever despises Me, despises Him Who sent me, My Father Who is in heaven."[2]

If we must honour the work and image of God even in mortal and sinful men, if we must honour the character of the Divine representative and envoy, even in the person of parents, princes, imperfect and even guilty priests,[3] what respect do we owe to those whom grace and glory have confirmed forever in the Divine friendship?

Honour the Saints: for them and through them God has done great things, and in turn, by God and for God, in the Name and for the glory of God, they have done great things. Give honour and love to the Saints: God honours and loves them; they honour God and they love Him.

But if among the creatures distinguished by holiness, that is to say by the irrevocable union with God, there is found one whom God has called to a superior rank, who has responded to the Divine choice with a more perfect fidelity, and who therefore was elevated above all that is not God, what honour do we not owe her!

This creature exists. Predestined from all eternity to be the Mother of God made man, Mary had been forewarned by a grace that raises her above all angels and all men taken together; to this super-

---

[2] "He that heareth you, heareth me; and he that despiseth you, despiseth me; and he that despiseth me, despiseth him that sent me." (Luke 10:16) "Amen, amen I say to you, he that receiveth whomsoever I send, receiveth Me; and he that receiveth Me, receiveth Him that sent Me." (John 13:20)

[3] I.e. priests who are also guilty sinners like us.

eminent grace she responded with a fidelity that places her virtue above all human and angelic virtues: finally the glory with which God crowned her fidelity to the grace of which He had forewarned her makes her the Queen of the angels and saints.

But if Mary outweighs all the saints in grace, virtue and glory, it is because she had to be and is the Mother of God made man, it is also because she had to be, and is indeed, the Mother of all the children of God, of all the elect.

So give honour and love to Mary: God honours and loves her, His Mother. Give honour and love to Mary: she honoured God, she loved Him, she honours and loves Him more than all the saints and all the angels put together. Give honour and love to Mary: she is our Mother; she wants to and can do us more good than all the angels. Give honour and love to Mary; after the worship due to God and to Jesus Christ His only Son, there is no devotion more legitimate and more salutary than that which is due to Mary, Mother of God and our Mother.

Notre-Dame de Chartres

Formerly, in the country of the Carnutes,[4] in the middle of an immense forest, rose a hill covered with a

---

[4] The Carnutes were a Gallic tribe that ruled a vast territory between the Seine and the Loire rivers during the Iron Age and the Roman period. Their name literally means 'the horned ones', which is thought to be a reference to their horned combat helmets. Chartres was named after them: in c. 400 it was called *Carnotum*, *Carnotis* in c. 650, and *Cartis* in 930 AD.

sacred wood which shaded a vast grotto. This was the religious centre of Gaul.[5] A hundred years before the birth of Jesus Christ, a great feast was celebrated in this place. On the altar of the grotto a statue had been placed representing a young girl who carried a newborn child in her arms. At the foot of the statue could be read these words. *Virgini pariturae,* 'To the Virgin who must be a mother' – the King of the Carnutes attended this solemnity with his warriors. The high priest addressed to them a speech in which he announced the birth of an extraordinary personage who was to save the world. There is nothing in this which should surprise us. Belief in the Virgin, Mother of the Universal Saviour, is found among all pagan peoples. The king of the Carnutes, whom legend designates by the Latin name of Priscus, was so touched by this speech that he consecrated his kingdom to the Future Mother of the Saviour. The assistants consecrated their persons to Him.[6]

Forty-six years after the birth of Jesus Christ, three envoys sent by St. Peter, Savinien, Potentien and Altinus, arrived in this country. At the sight of the statue and the prophetic inscription *Virgini pariturae,*

---

5   I.e. the ancient Roman word for the region that is now France.

6   There is another account which states a miracle that happened in the grotto is what caused King Priscus to dedicate his kingdom to the Virgin. The son of one of the great chieftains had fallen into a well and had drowned. The father took the body of his child, mounted his charger, riding liking the wind for twenty leagues, he approached the druid altar of the Virgin and laid the boy at her feet. He came back to life and and smiled at the sacred statue. On hearing this, King Priscus summoned a great assembly of priests and nobles, and appointed the Lady his heiress and the Queen of his realms. (Source: Chapter I: Druids and Romans: The Crypt' in *'The Story of Chartres',* by Cecil Headlam. J.M Dent and Co, London, 1902.)

Chartres

they were happily surprised. They announced to the Carnutes the arrival of Him whose Mother they had already honoured for a century and a half. The grotto was consecrated to Mary. This is where today stands the splendid Cathedral of Notre Dame de Chartres. Thus, even before she existed, Mary had taken possession of Gaul, which was to be France one day.

☙ ❀ ❧

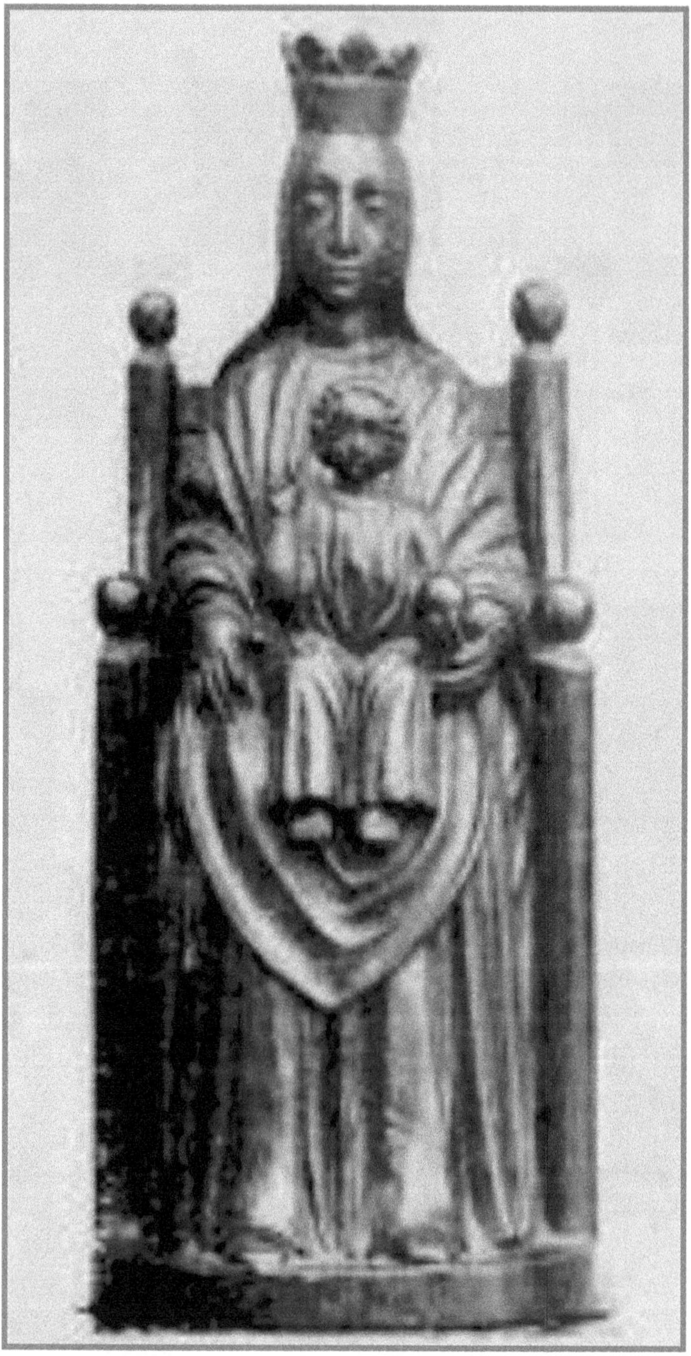

Above: Chapel of of Our Lady Sous Terre at Chartres on the site of the ancient grotto.

Left: Wood replica of the ancient statue of the Virgin Mother with Child dating from the 17th century.

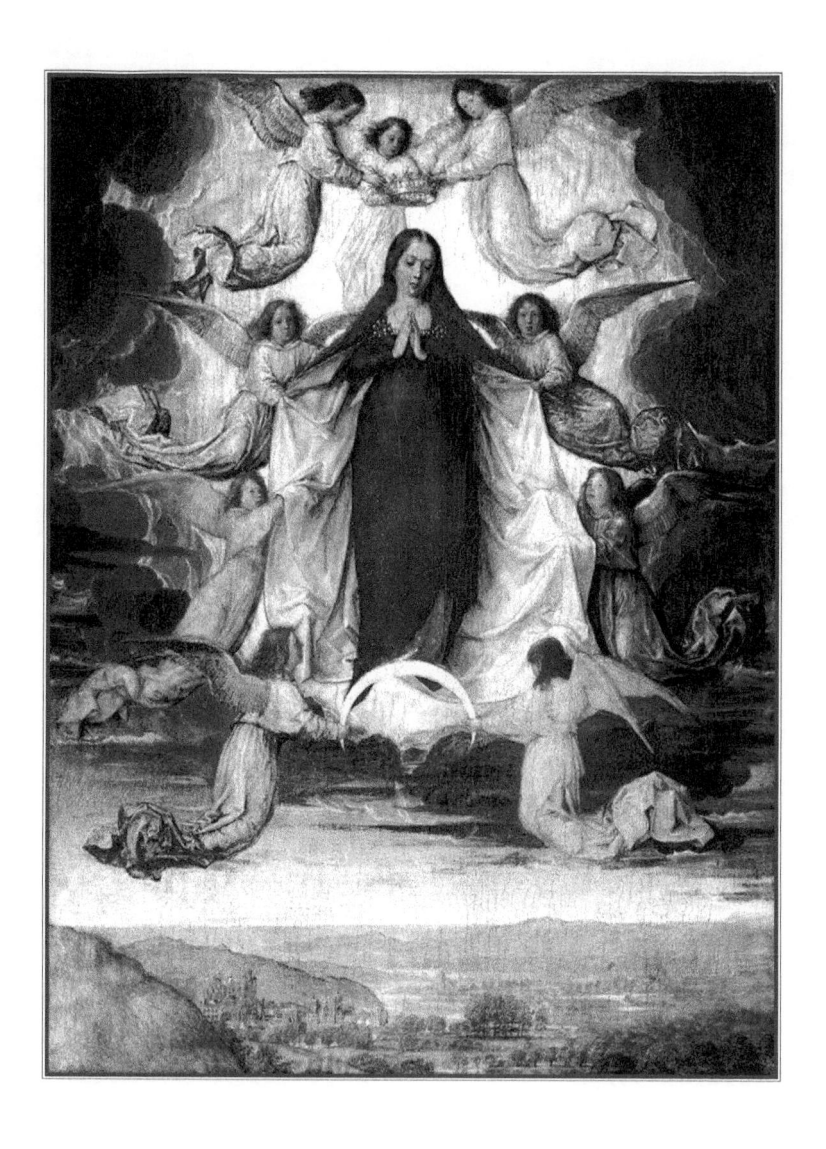

2 ~ The Greatness of Mary

The greatness of Mary must be measured by the grace God has given her, by her faithfulness in corresponding to that grace, and by the glory with which God has rewarded her faithfulness.

The grace of which God reserved for Mary can be reduced to three counts:

First: predestination to the Divine Maternity; this grace is the foundation and the reason for all the other privileges which will distinguish Mary from the rest of Creation;

Second: preservation from Original sin: consequence of the preceding grace;

Third: a miraculous birth, as everything had to be extraordinary in her who, without ceasing to be a virgin, was to be the Mother of the Son of God.

The virtue of Mary, her correspondence to grace is shown above all in three circumstances:

First: on the day of her presentation to the Temple, when at the age of three she consecrated herself to God, and that by this gift of her person and of her life, she responds so fully to the miraculous benefit of her birth.

Second: on the day of the Annunciation, when, by accepting the burdens and pains attached to the honour of the Divine Motherhood, she co-responds to the privilege of her Immaculate Conception, to extend it in some way to the entire human race, which although not preserved from original sin like her, can at least be delivered from it by He Whom she is going to give to the world;

Third: at the day of her Purification, when she

presents her Divine Son to the Heavenly Father, and, already sacrificing Him for the salvation of the world, she responds generously to the singular grace of the Divine Motherhood.

God cannot allow Himself to be outdone in generosity: His dignity is in agreement with His goodness and defends it. God cannot leave His work unfinished: wisdom and honour do not allow Him to. By His grace He laid down the principle of the greatness of Mary; by her virtue Mary responded to this grace; by glory, God will crown this masterpiece of grace and virtue.

To the honour of the Divine Motherhood Mary responded by returning to the Heavenly Father her Divine Son through the sacrifice begun on the day of the Purification, and consummated on the cross. The dying Jesus gives as sons to His Mother all the elect represented by the beloved disciple. (This is) Mary's First Glory: Universal Maternity.

Preserved from Original sin in view of the Divine Maternity, Mary accepted all the sacrifices attached to this glorious privilege and this incomparable dignity; God will not allow the immaculate body which was the living temple of the Incarnate Word to remain in the tomb. Thus the second glory of Mary: her glorious Assumption.

Recognizing the miracle of her birth, Mary presented herself at the Temple to consecrate her person and her life there to God. God rewards such generous humility by crowning her Queen of Heaven and earth. The third glory of Mary: Universal Royalty.

From this triple consideration on the greatness of Mary, I deduce a triple conclusion, a triple practical application:

First: without God we can do nothing; without His grace there is neither virtue nor greatness;

Second: But without us, without virtue, without a generous and constant effort on our part to correspond to the Divine advances, grace remains powerless to sanctify and save us. This is the thought of St. Augustine: "God could well have created us without us, but He will not save us without us and in spite of us."

Third: God owes to His wisdom and justice to complete what He began in us and what we have pursued with His help; and it is our duty to crown His work and ours, His grace and our virtue, with a glory that surpasses even the most singular grace and even the most heroic virtue.

We have recalled the titles of Mary's greatness, we have thereby shown Mary's rights to a special and superior devotion which is called the devotion of *hyperdulia*;[7] we will next say how this devotion can be rendered to her.

---

[7] There are distinct forms of devotion: 1) Latria: an act of adoration or worship due to God (the Holy Trinity) alone and no other, e.g. the Mass, 2) Hyperdulia: the respect and veneration due the Mother of God, full of grace and higher than any other created creature, 3) Protodulia: the respect and veneration due St. Joseph, the greatest saint after the Blessed Virgin on account of having been specially chosen to guard her and provide for her as his spouse, and of course, for being chosen to become the earthly foster father of the Saviour, guarding Him and also raising Him as his own, 4) Dulia, the devotion and respect towards the rest of the saints.

The Veil of Mary

Eight centuries pass. It seems that Mary did not cease during this long time to show her power and her goodness at Chartres, because in 876 AD, the King of France, Charles-le-Chauve, took from the church of Notre Dame d'Aix-la-Chapel one of the two tunics of the Blessed Virgin that Charlemagne had placed there, and donated it to Notre Dame de Chartres. This distinction seems to prove then that no other sanctuary in France was more worthy of receiving such a precious treasure.

This tunic is rather a veil. Women in the Orient wore, instead of a chemise, a long piece of cloth which covered the head, crossed over the chest, folded under the arms and enveloped the whole upper part of the body. The veil which is preserved at Chartres is four and a half ells long.[8] It is a yellowish-white linen and silk fabric. This garment is doubly venerable; first, as it was in contact with the virginal body of Mary, and, according to tradition, the Blessed Virgin carried it during all the time that the Divine Child remained in her womb.

According to Nicephorus Callixtus (Hist. Eccl. Liv. XIV, c. II. Et book XV, c. XIV) this veil was left to a friend by the dying Virgin. Then it fell into the hands of a Jew from Galilee. Around the fifth century, two brothers named Candidus and Galbius obtained it from this Jew. Wanting to ensure the preservation of this treasure, they kept it carefully hidden, but the secret

---

[8] An ell is 45 inches long. The veil would be about 202.5 inches, or about 514.35 cm.

The Relic of the Veil at Chartres

was betrayed by miracles. To receive such a relic with dignity, Emperor Leo, known as the Great or the Elder, had a magnificent temple built.

In 810 Emperor Nicephorus and Empress Irene[9] presented it to Charlemagne along with another garment of the Blessed Virgin. The pious emperor deposited them in his dear church of Our Lady of Aix-la-Chapelle, from where the veil of which we have just spoken was transferred by Charles-le-Chauve to Our Lady of Chartres.

---

9 The emperor's full name was Constantine Porphyrogenitus.

Then came the time of the Norman invasions. One day in 911 AD, Chartres saw with horror the terrible Rollo camped under its walls. The battle begins; already the Normans are victorious. But at the height of the fray the Bishop of Chartres appeared.[10] Dressed in pontifical vestments, he carried a spear in his hand. From this spear hung a banner of a new kind; it is the veil of the Virgin Mary. At this sight, Rollo feels seized with a fear of which he had not known until then; the Normans withdrew, but in good order, showing that they yielded rather to a supernatural ascendancy than to the valour of their adversaries.

The Chartrains, filled with gratitude, erected a chapel to their liberator in the very ravine occupied by the enemy army. This place since was called *Valrollon*, or *Vauroux* (by corruption of the word).

---

10   Bishop Gantelme did this heroic act.

View of Chartres

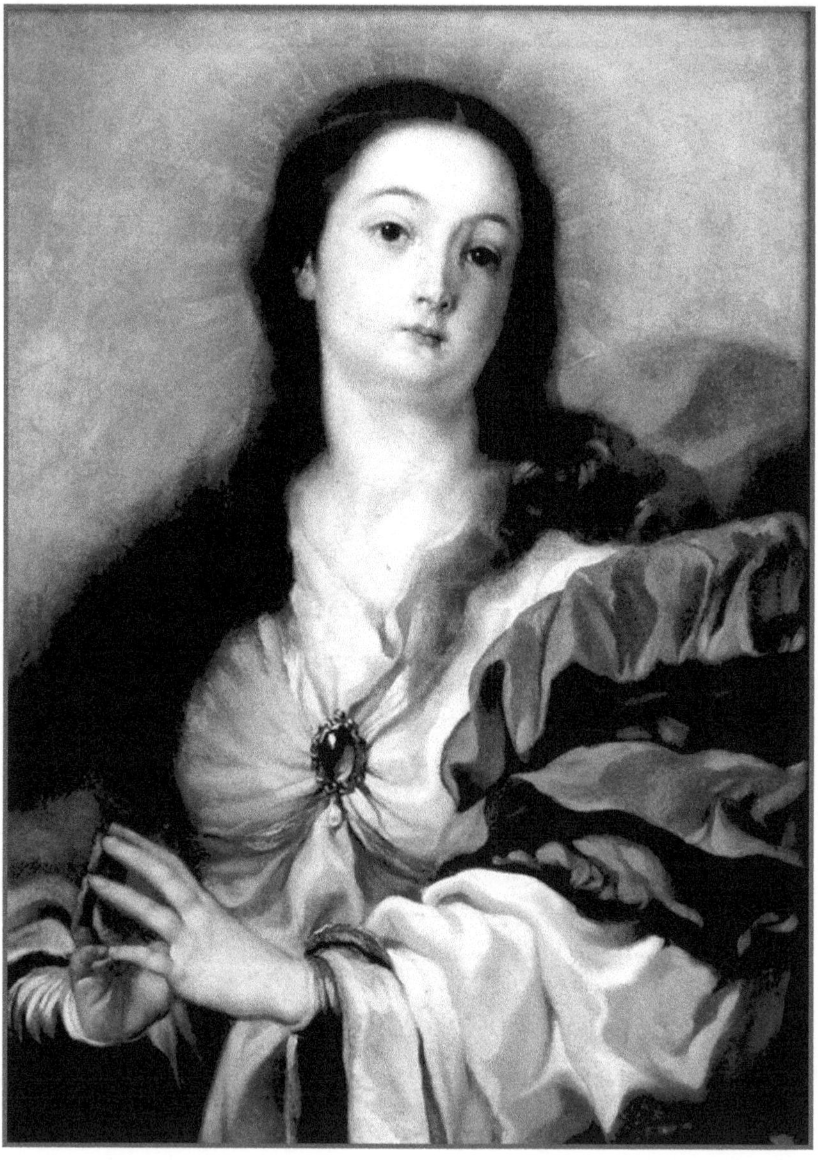

3 ~ **Devotion to Mary**

Three words sum up the devotion we owe to Mary: First: imitation, Second: veneration, Third: invocation.

Imitation

Let us imitate Mary: she is the Mother of Jesus, she is our Mother.

God became man, God made Himself like unto us, so that it would be possible for us to imitate Him and become similar to Him. But if Jesus is a man like us, He is also God; His perfection is human, no doubt, but at the same time it is Divine. This model is hopeless (to resemble). Lower your gaze a little, rest it on Mary. Like you, Mary is a simple creature; imitate her, you will nevertheless be like Jesus.

For it is a law of nature by virtue of which, generally, a son resembles his father and mother. Consider Jesus. As God, He is the consubstantial image of the Father, the reflection, the splendour of His glory. As a man, He is the image of His mother. But here the very order demands that the rule be reversed. It is for the more perfect and not for the less perfect to serve as a type. Mary therefore had to be moulded beforehand on the type of Jesus, and so at His entry into the world, Jesus, although incomparably more perfect, found Himself similar to His Mother, who on her side, in order to become more more similar to her Son, never ceased from the moment of the birth of the Divine Child to contemplate this perfect Model, to study It, to compare It, to preserve all Its features, and to reproduce them in her own life: *Maria autem conservabat omnia verba haec, conferens in cord suo.* ("Mary kept all these words, pondering them in her heart." Luke 2:19) So let us imitate Mary, Mother of Jesus, she is similar to Jesus. If we will resemble the Mother, we will resemble the Son.

She is also our Mother. Let us imitate her if we want her to recognize us as her children. Let us imitate her in order to resemble her First born, if we want her to find in us the brothers of Jesus.

The Kings and Notre Dame de Chartres

It is not surprising that Notre Dame de Chartres now enjoys an ever-growing celebrity. Among the kings of France, there are few who have not come to pay homage there. Let us first name Eudes, Robert-la-Pieux, Henry I, Philippe I.

Louis VI, called 'the Fat', (1118), was at war with Thibaut IV. Chartres obeyed his enemy, but the King dared not attack the city of Mary. He could have entered as a conqueror, but he presented himself as a pilgrim and prostrated himself at the feet of the ancient statue.

The conqueror of Bouvines, Philippe-Augustus, who owed this victory to the protection of Mary, soon had to thank Our Lady of Chartres for a no less signal favour. Philippe had no heir, therefore his wife Isabelle came to Chartres. She was praying there before the image of the Virgin Mother, when suddenly four candles lit themselves. (*Source: Guillaue le Breton*). She had a son who reigned as Louis VIII called "the Lion".

Louis-le-Lion's wife, Blanche de Castille, was also struck with sterility. She came to pray in the grotto and God gave her several sons. The eldest was St. Louis. Chartres will see him twice prostrated at the feet of the image of She who was doubly his mother: his mother as a Christian, his mother by the miracle of his birth.

The French and the Flemmish were at grips at Mons-en-Puelle (August 17, 1304). Philippe-le-Bel, strongly pressed by the enemy, invoked Our Lady of Chartres, and he escaped death. To fulfil the vow he had made at the time of danger, he came to Chartres mounted on the same war horse and wearing the same arms as on the day of the battle and he paid homage by giving the armour and the courier to She who gave him victory.

Twenty four years later (August 23, 1328), Philippe de Valois again won a signal victory over the same enemies at Mont-Cassel. Again the valour of the Flemish forced the French king to invoke Mary. The winner made homage of his triumph to Our Lady of Paris, but the testimony of his gratitude would have seemed to him incomplete if he had not come to renew this expression at the feet of Our Lady of Chartres.

King Jean visited Chartres three times, bearing the humble staff of the pilgrim. But the hour of the test had sounded for France; the disastrous battle of Poitiers handed it over to the English.

The Dauphin, who was since Charles V the Wise, made the pilgrimage to Chartres barefoot; Mary would show herself. ...

Everywhere victorious until then, the English Edouard III arrived in front of Chartres (1360). The locals turned to the Blessed Virgin. Suddenly a terrible storm burst on the camp of the English. The tents were

Chartres cathedral (c. 1830s)

overturned, the weapons and the luggage were washed away by the waters, enormous hailstones fall on the army. Already a thousand men-at-arms and six thousand horses had perished. Edward then turns to the cathedral, he kneels down and grants peace to France. Instantly the hurricane subsides. Shortly afterwards peace was signed at Brétigny, near Chartres.

Our Lady of Chartres had already given two kings to France, Louis VIII 'the Lion' and Louis IX the Saint, she will take under her high protection a branch of the family of Saint Louis who will one day elevate the kingdom to the highest and most Christian degree.

It was during the reign of Charles VI: one day they saw one hundred knights entering Chartres who, each holding in his hand not the sword but a lighted candle, came to present themselves at the door of the cathedral. Louis de Bourbon, Comte de Vendôme, barefoot, humbly followed this brilliant procession. Arriving at the royal gate, the prince knelt on the steps, he tells of how Mary delivered him from the hands of Jacques, his brother, who held him in harsh captivity. Then he rises, he declares himself her servant, it is from this illustrious branch that the kings will come out of which Henri IV will be the first.

Louis XII, Francis I, Francis II, Charles IX, Henry III, made the pilgrimage to Chartres. But action must answer prayer. These kings forgot that their first duty was to maintain the royalty of the Son of Mary. Louis XII clashed with the Pope; he died without issue. The other three by their negligence allowed heresy to creep into France. Under Henry III it (heresy) would walk with its head raised, also threatening religion and royalty. Fortunately Our Lady of Chartres was keeping watch.

4 ~ **Veneration**

Mary is the Mother of Jesus, she is our Mother. She is the Mother of Jesus. And Jesus, all great, God though He is, honours her as His Mother. She is our Mother: a Mother with a right to receive homage from her children.

Jesus honours Mary as His Mother. For her, and for her alone, He did more than for the whole world. Of the thirty-three years He passed on this earth, thirty are consecrated to Mary; three will suffice for the rest of mankind. It is true that all the time devoted to Mary is thereby devoted to us. Completing the perfection of His Mother, Jesus formed for us a Mother.

Jesus honours Mary as His Mother. He wants everything to be held in common between Her and Him. And first of all, if there is no salvation except in Jesus and through Jesus, I do not see how one can separate Mary from Jesus. No one will be saved if he does not believe in Jesus Christ, if he does not believe that Jesus Christ is truly God and truly man. But if you do not believe that Mary is truly the Mother of a Son Who is God and man, if you do not believe that the only Son of God was incarnated and conceived in the womb of the Virgin Mary and He was born from this most pure Mother, you do not believe in the Word made flesh, in God made man, *you do not believe in Jesus Christ*. Also, in the Creed, faith in the Divine Motherhood of Mary is inseparable from faith in the Incarnation: *Credo ... in Jesum Christim Filium ejus (Dei Patris) unicum ... qui ... natus ex Mari Virgine.* ("I believe ... in Jesus Christ His (God the Father's)

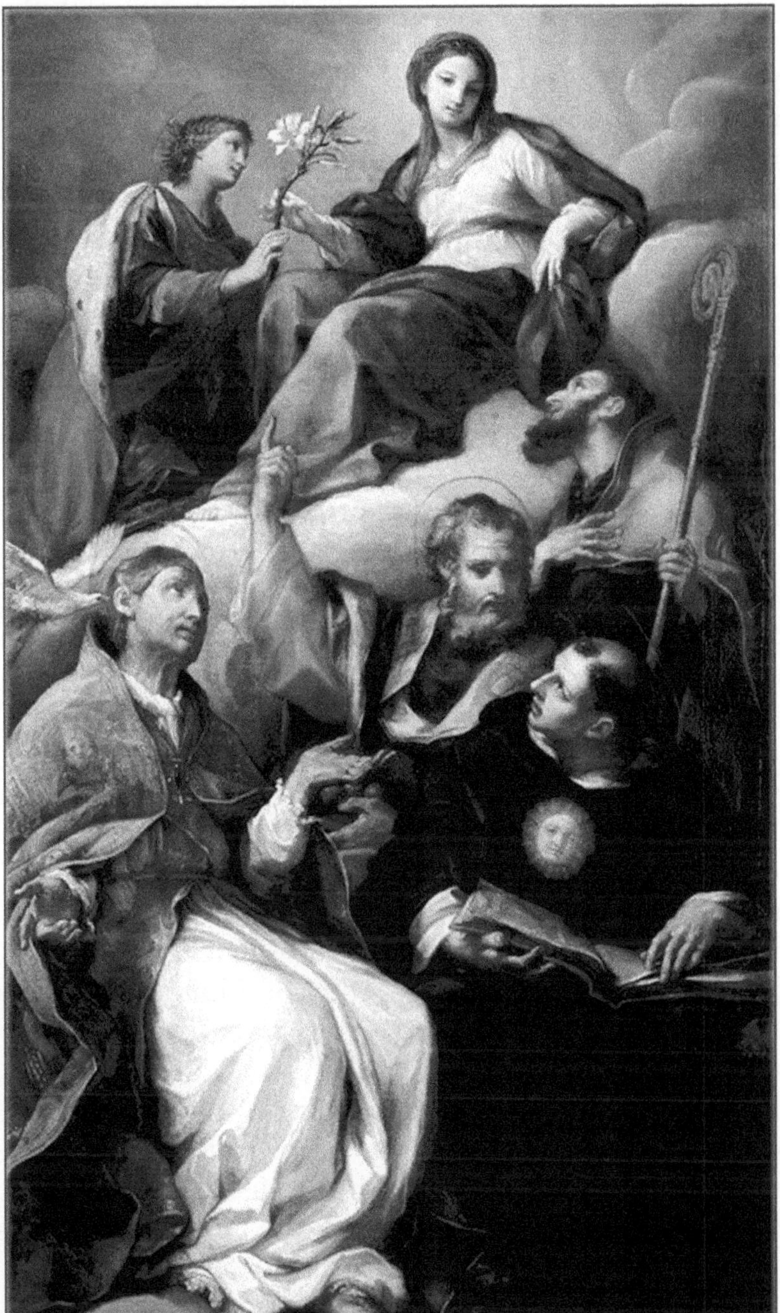

only Son ... Who ... was born of the Virgin Mary."

Should we then be surprised at the (similar) honours that Jesus, immaculate and impeccable by nature, grants Mary who is immaculate and impeccable by grace? Virgin Jesus, Virgin Mary. Jesus was pierced by an exterior lance, Mary is pierced by an interior sword. Jesus, incorruptible in the tomb, resurrected on the third day by His own virtue; Mary, preserved from the corruption of the sepulchre, was resurrected on the third day by the virtue of her Divine Son. Jesus rose up to heaven body and soul, Mary also was raised up.

The Church, by wanting to venerate Mary, the Mother of Jesus and our Mother, does not separate her from her Son.

It equally encourages the invocation of the sacred Name of Jesus and of the holy name of Mary.

One will hardly find a temple without a chapel, an altar dedicated to Mary, or at least an image of Mary.

To each feast in honour of the Son corresponds a feast in honour of the Mother. If we celebrate the Incarnation of the Word, that is to say the Conception of Jesus, we celebrate the Conception of Mary. We honour the Nativity of Jesus and that of Mary. We celebrate the holy Names of Jesus and Mary, the Presentation of Jesus and that of Mary, the Sacred Heart of Jesus and the Immaculate Heart of Mary.

Following the example of Jesus, the example of the Church, we venerate Mary. Venture to venerate her, you will always fall below what you owe her; never will your efforts, never will your excesses correspond to the dignity of your Mother, of the Mother of Jesus: *Quantum potes tantum aude, quia major omni laude, nec laudare sufficis.*[11] If some narrow and chagrined soul is scandalized by your audacity, answer that if this honour, if this praise seems excessive for Mary, it is not so according to her Son: *si Mariae not congruent, congruit Filio ejus.*

The Protestants and Our Lady of Chartres

In 1568, at the height of the wars of religion, Condé with the Huguenots came to besiege the city of Mary. Putting all their confidence in the Virgin other inhabitants placed her statue on each of the gates with this inscription: *Carnutum tutela,* defence of the Chartrains. The heretics opened fire against the Drouese gate, and it was at the image of Mary that these impious aimed their blows; but were unable to reach it. However, a section of wall collapsed. The soldiers of the city faced the enemy, the population rushed into the grotto to the feet of the Virgin Mother. Suddenly, without knowing why, instead of taking advantage of the breach in the wall, the Huguenots withdrew and lifted the siege. The Chartrains recognized the help of Our Lady in this inexplicable retreat and, to perpetuate the memory of their gratitude, they built a chapel in honour of Our Lady de

---

11 "All thou canst, do thou endeavour: / Yet thy praise can equal never / Such as merits thy great King," from the *Lauda Sion*, the sequence composed by St. Thomas Aquinas for the Mass of *Corpus Christi*. The example here: if we can never praise the Son enough, we also cannot praise His most pure Mother as much as she deserves.

Siege of Chartres

Note the breach in the wall, centre background.

la Brèche in front of the section of wall shot down by the Huguenot cannon.

Finally, thanks to the zeal of Catholic France, Henry IV understood that he would never be King of the French if he is not the most Christian king. He had himself instructed and abjured heresy, and it was at Notre Dame de Chartres, on the rood screen of the splendid cathedral, that he wanted to receive the royal coronation.

It is therefore at the feet of Our Lady of Chartres that France's three most formidable enemies fell.

There, stopped the last pagan invaders of French soil, the Normans of Rollo who, repulsed by the arm of Mary before Chartres, were not long in becoming Christians.

There, struck down by Mary, the English were forced to grant a peace without which France would have become English, and later perhaps Protestant.

There, repulsed by the image of Mary, the Protestants see their hopes and their pretensions disappointed by the coronation of Henry IV, who became the Most Christian King.

We are not yet at the end of the favours granted by Our Lady of Chartres.

꧁❀꧂

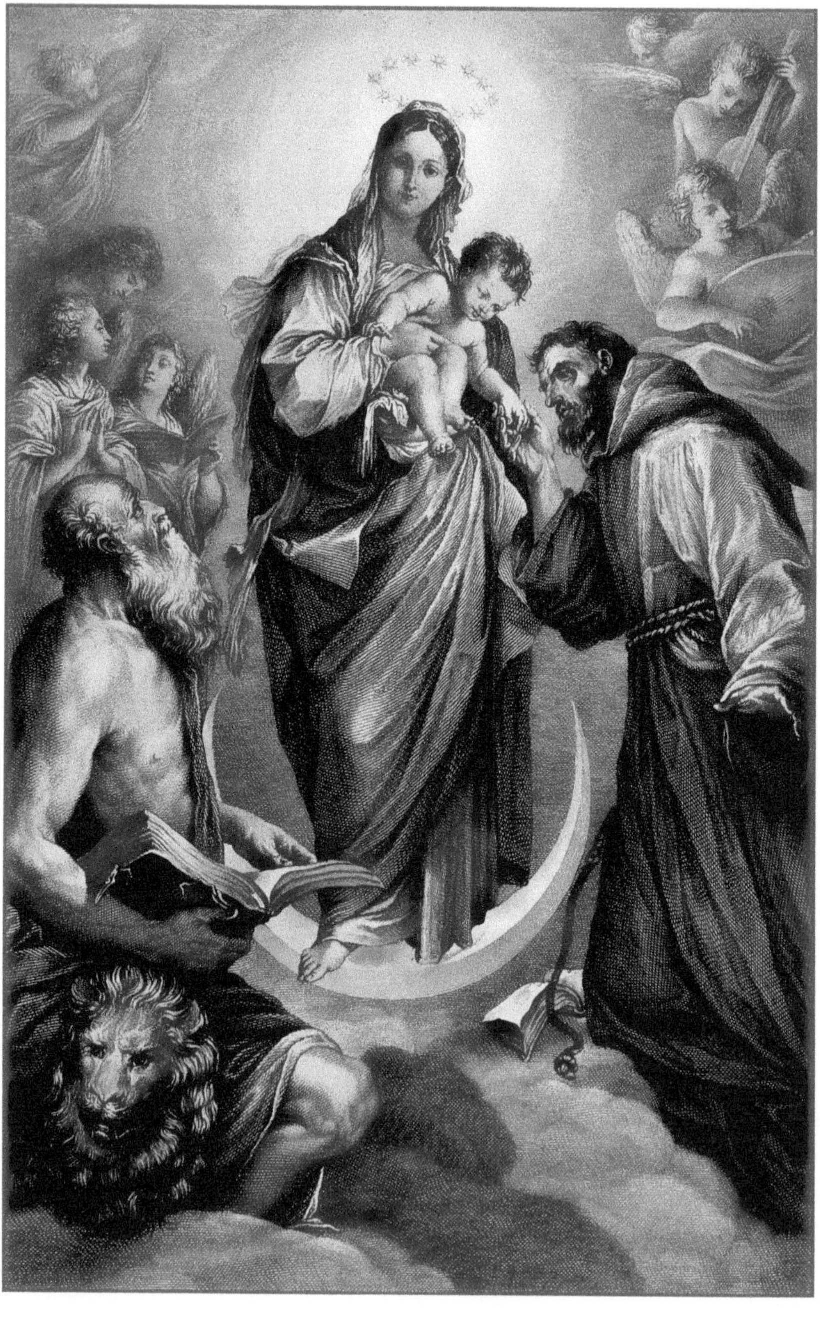

5 ~ **Invocation**

Let us go to the Father through the Son; let us go to the Son through the Mother. Such is the will of God Who willed us to have everything entirely through Mary; *Quia sic est voluntas Dei qui totum nos habere voluit per Mariam.* (St. Bernard)

Mother of Jesus, Mary is most powerful to aid us, but she is also completely benevolent because she is our Mother. She is good because she is a Mother, she is strong because she is Queen.

Child of a Mother so tender, soldier of a Queen so great, do you wish to assure yourself of her royal maternal protection? Join her army, put on her armour, and learn to wield her weapons.

Mary's army is the Congregation. One engages in it by a special consecration to her service and by the promise to defend her honour and her interests against the attacks of impiety and license. The disbelievers and the libertines ganged up against faith and virtue. At this sight, the children of God united under the invocation of the Immaculate Virgin, under the Virgin Mary, the Queen of the Angels, and so the Congregation was formed. You can understand then why impiety honours the Congregation by its hatred and its fury through persecution of it. But also understand these words from a great saint of modern times: "When a layman asks me what he must do to be saved, I cannot advise him of a more useful and safer way than to enter the Congregation. The Congregation is a means which includes all the others, even the most infallible, for eternal salvation." (St. Alphonsus de

Liguori).[12]

Enrol on the registers of the Archconfraternity of the Most Holy and Immaculate Heart of Mary, established at Notre Dame des Victories in Paris for the conversion of sinners.[13] By this inscription you will be in union of prayer with the twenty million associates of this peaceful league. Add the recitation of an *Ave Maria*, even if it were only that of your morning or evening prayer, for the intention of the Archconfraternity: you have fulfilled all the obligations that it proposes to its members.

---

[12] I.e. a confraternity, or archconfraternity is meant here. However, it appears there is a confusion as to which confraternity St. Alphonsus was referring to, especially as the confraternity mentioned by Fr. de Boylesve in this and the next paragraph was formed in the 1830s years after St. Alphonsus' death (August 1, 1787). I cannot find this particular quote attributed him, although he was known to promote several confraternities of Our Lady for the assurance of eternal salvation. The Holy Rosary Archconfraternity was one. Of course, there can be no greater assurance of salvation through Mary's help other than praying the rosary than by joining the Brown Scapular Archconfraternity and wearing the Brown Scapular.

[13] The Archconfraternity of the Most Holy and Immaculate Heart of Mary for the Conversion of Sinners founded in 1836 by the parish priest of Our Lady of Victories, Paris. In 1838 it was raised to an archconfraternity with the right of expanding throughout the world. The special veneration of the Immaculate Heart of Mary is the first aim of the confraternity, and is also the principle means of attaining the second aim, which is the conversion of sinners. The confraternity has had considerable success with regards to conversions. The original branch in Paris still exists today and one may enroll online. See their site for more information, (French required):
www.notredamedesvictoires.com/archiconfrerie/

Notre Dame de Chartres after Louis XIII

The son of Henry the Great, Louis XIII, from the first days of his reign came himself to Chartres to place his person and his crown under the protection of the Virgin. It thus was a prelude to the solemn act which was to consecrate France to Mary in the church of Notre Dame de Paris.

Like Isabelle once before, and like Blanche of Castile, Anne of Austria descended into the venerated grotto to ask the Virgin Mother for a son. Finally, after twenty-two years of sterility, she gave birth to an infant who would be Louis XIV.

France therefore owes Notre Dame de Chartres three of its kings: Louis the Lion, St. Louis, and Louis the Great.

Louis XIV was not ungrateful. It was to the assistance of She who is terrible as an army in battle array that he attributed the victories gained by his great captains, and several times he made the pilgrimage to Chartres to venerate his powerful Protector and his beloved Mother.

Then came the days of desolation.

How the cathedral of Notre Dame de Chartres was able to come through almost intact after the destructive hurricane that the Revolution had unleashed upon all the sacred monuments, no one knows. Be that as it may, Mary had not abandoned the city of her predilections. She showed it clearly when in 1832 cholera began its ravages there.[14] In just a few

---

14   This was during the second world-wide cholera pandemic of 1826-1837. Also known as the Asiatic cholera

days, one hundred and sixty people had succumbed. On the Sunday of August 26, the reliquary containing the venerated veil was carried in procession. Two individuals took the liberty of insulting the piety of the faithful. They also laughed at the cholera outbreak; but, suddenly seized by the scourge, they expired in dreadful contortions. They were the last victims; yet by the procession, not one other inhabitant died of cholera.[15]

From all these facts and a thousand others that we silently pass over, would it not be permissible to infer that Notre Dame de Chartres can also be called Notre Dame de France? Chartres is like the capital of our August Queen, and this temple, this marvel of art, this lapidary epic, to borrow the expression of an orator of this century, is her palace.

But following the example of the queens of the earth, the Queen of Heaven likes to visit the provinces of her kingdom, and everywhere she has palaces, privileged sanctuaries that she honours with her most special favour. We will follow her to some of these blessed places.

൚ ⚜ ൞

---

pandemic, it reached from India across Western Asia into Europe, spread to Great Britain, and the Americas, as well as spreading east to China and Japan. Several more world wide pandemics would break out, cholera was the scourge of the 19th century and caused more deaths than any other epidemic disease.

15   Cecil Headlam also notes a medal was struck in 1832 commemorating this event. Not one inhabitant who was ill died, except the two who dared to mock the procession. (*'The Story of Chartres'*, *by* Cecil Headlam. J.M Dent and Co, London, 1902.)

Assumption of the Virgin – statue at the altar at Chartres

6 ~ The Armour of Mary

The armour of Mary consists, if you will, of three main pieces: the scapular, her medal, her image.

Put on the brown scapular; it will be for you the breastplate of justice, faith and charity of which St. Paul speaks. (Ephes. 6:14 and 1 Thess. 5:8).[16] Mary promised that he who died covered with this holy livery would be preserved from the fires of hell: *In quo quis morien aeternum non patietur incendium.* Whether you preserve yourself from sin, or remove yourself from it by perfect contrition or by confession, Mary will be faithful to her promise. But beware: if you count sin as nothing, if you make yourself a slave to passion or human respect, if you give yourself up to indifference, to unbelief, to impiety, what will you do with the scapular? You will leave it, you will forget it, you will reject it, and you will force Mary to leave you and forget you in her turn.

To the scapular of Carmel add that of the Immaculate Conception, and pray for the reformation of morals and the conversion of sinners.[17] This practice gives the right to gain the (plenary) indulgences of Jerusalem, of the seven basilicas of Rome, of the Portiuncula and of St. James of Compostella, without

---

[16]   "Stand therefore, having your loins girt about with truth, and having on the breastplate of justice," (Ephes. 6:14) "But let us, who are of the day, be sober, having on the breastplate of faith and charity, and for a helmet the hope of salvation." (1 Thess. 5:)

[17]   Scapular of the Immaculate Conception: I.e. the Blue Scapular. (See Appendix 2 for more information about this scapular.)

the need for confession and Communion, all the times that six Paters, Aves at Glorias are recited in honour of the Holy Trinity and the Immaculate Conception and for the intentions of the Pope.[18]

Carry a medal of Mary, especially the Miraculous Medal. It will serve as a shield to repel the enemy's fiery darts. (Eph. 6:16)[19]

Finally, may the image of Mary always be displayed in some place where your eyes can easily encounter it. It will be like a banner, the presence of which will constantly remind you of your commitments.

Mary in Paris

On the left bank of the Seine in the middle of the fields, it is said there was raised a temple consecrated to Ceres.[20] It is reported that St. Denis, having come to preach the Gospel in Paris, purified this temple and dedicated it to the devotion of Mary, who was honoured there under the title of Notre Dame des

---

[18] **NOTE:** apparently, this particular concession of gaining plenary indulgences without the other requirements of confession and Communion before saying each of the six prayers is no longer part of the indulgence privileges. As with other plenary indulgences granted to the faithful, the requirements for plenary indulgences granted to Blue Scapular members requires Communion and confession. See Appendix 2 for the updated rules.

[19] "In all things taking the shield of faith, wherewith you may be able to extinguish all the fiery darts of the most wicked one." (Eph. 6:16)

[20] Ceres: the Roman goddess of agriculture, grain crops, fertility, and motherly or maternal relationships.

*The Carmelite convent
on what was once called the Rue d'Enfer*

(c. 1860s)

Champs.[21]

St. Denis had seen the most holy Virgin, and he had been so struck by the majesty of her person, that if faith had not restrained him, he would have prostrated himself at her feet to adore her. He brought to Gaul a portrait of the August Virgin, which was kept for a long time in the church of Notre Dame de Champs. This oratory has lost its old name, it is now the chapel of the Carmelite convent at the Rue d'Enfer.[22]

During the invasion of the Franks, Paris was almost entirely included on the island still called the Cité today. There was a temple of Druids there. It was on the site of this building that Clovis, who became a Christian, laid the first stone of a church which, after more than one transformation, became the majestic basilica of Notre Dame de Paris. The first construction was completed by Childebert.

We can therefore say that from then on, Mary had taken possession of the future capital of France. She will know how to defend it.

In 885 AD, Sigfred with thirty thousand Normans came to besiege Paris, which then already extended on both banks of the river. To reach the

---

21 According to tradition, he drove demons from the temple of Ceres before dedicating it to the Blessed Virgin under the title Notre Dame des Champs, Our Lady of the Fields.

22 The street is no longer called Rue d'Enfer, but Rue Henri-Barbusse. This second Carmel at Rue Henri-Barbusse was abolished in 1906 and only the memory of it remained through the name of the street, the Rue Notre-Dame-des-Champs, and also by the new church of Notre-Dame des Champs that was built a kilometer away from the original site on the Boulevard du Montparnasse.

walls, the barbarians filled the ditches with the corpses of the prisoners and prepared to cross this human bridge. At this sight, outraged with pain, Bishop Gozlin [23] raised his eyes to heaven, invoked Mary, then seizing a bow he shot an arrow at Sigfred and struck him down dead. Disconcerted by the fall of their leader, the Normans fled. Paris is saved. Mary's image was processed in triumph through the streets and received the homage of public recognition.

ଛ ✤ ଓ

---

23 Unfortunately, this might be a romantic embellishment of the siege. According to "Paris and its Story by Thomas Okey, the bishop entered the fray with bow and axe to defend Paris, and his nephew joined him. Even though wounded by a javelin strike early on in the attack, the Bishop succeeded in bringing down a great chieftain with an arrow, but Sigfred isn't named. The chieftain's body was thrown into the human bridge with the rest of the dead. The attack continued, and despite their advances, the enemies were 'baffled' by the courage of the defenders of Paris and forced to draw back and make another attempt at taking the city, this time with doubled fury. The Bishop then invoked Our Lady, under title Maris Stella, Star of the sea to save them from the cruelty of the Danes, but the battle was not yet over. And the Bishop did not live to see the end of the siege. However, the enemies suddenly stopped their attack on the city, having been bribed off for the winter at least until they attempted a new attack. Seeing the raiders once come by boat, it was an abbot named Ebles, who with a well aimed bow shot, struck the pilot dead, terrifying the raiders who agreed to a treaty not to ravage the Marne. Eventually the city enjoyed peace for a spell. Despite the mix up in details, no doubt Our Lady protected the city and spared it from falling judging by the sudden and inexplicable fright caused by the one arrow strike. (Source; Chapter 3 in "Paris and its Story" by Thomas Okey, J.M. Dent and Co. London, 1904).

Notre Dame, Paris (c. 1860s)

7 ~ The Weapons of Mary

By the arms of Mary I mean what St. Paul calls the sword of the spirit or the word of God. (*Gladium spiritus qud est verbum Dei.* - Ephes. 6:17) ("And take unto you the helmet of salvation, and the sword of the Spirit (which is the word of God.)

First of all, it is the holy name of Mary. Invoke her unceasingly, especially in danger, especially in temptation. *Maria cogita, Mariam invoca* – Think of Mary, invoke Mary. May this name, so sweet and so powerful, always be on your lips, always in your heart: *Non recedat ab ore, no recedat a corde.* (St. Bernard).

The Angelic Salutation (the Hail Mary), after the Pater (the Our Father), is the prayer *par excellence.* It recalls the Incarnation of the Word and the Divine Maternity of the Virgin, a double mystery which supposes and which also recalls both the Trinity of the Divine Persons and the Immaculate Conception of Mary. The Trinity: the Father sent the Son, the Son was made incarnate in Mary's womb by the operation of the Holy Spirit. The Immaculate Conception, through which Mary is full of grace, *gratia plena*; and is inseparable from the Lord, *Dominus tecum, (the Lord is with Thee),* and therefore is blessed among women; *benedicta tu in mulieribus*; here is the Immaculate Conception, without which Mary would not have been worthy of becoming the Mother of a God. This prayer sums up the whole Christian religion.

We also find there (in the Ave Maria) the holy names of Jesus and Mary.

The first part was inspired by the Holy Spirit and

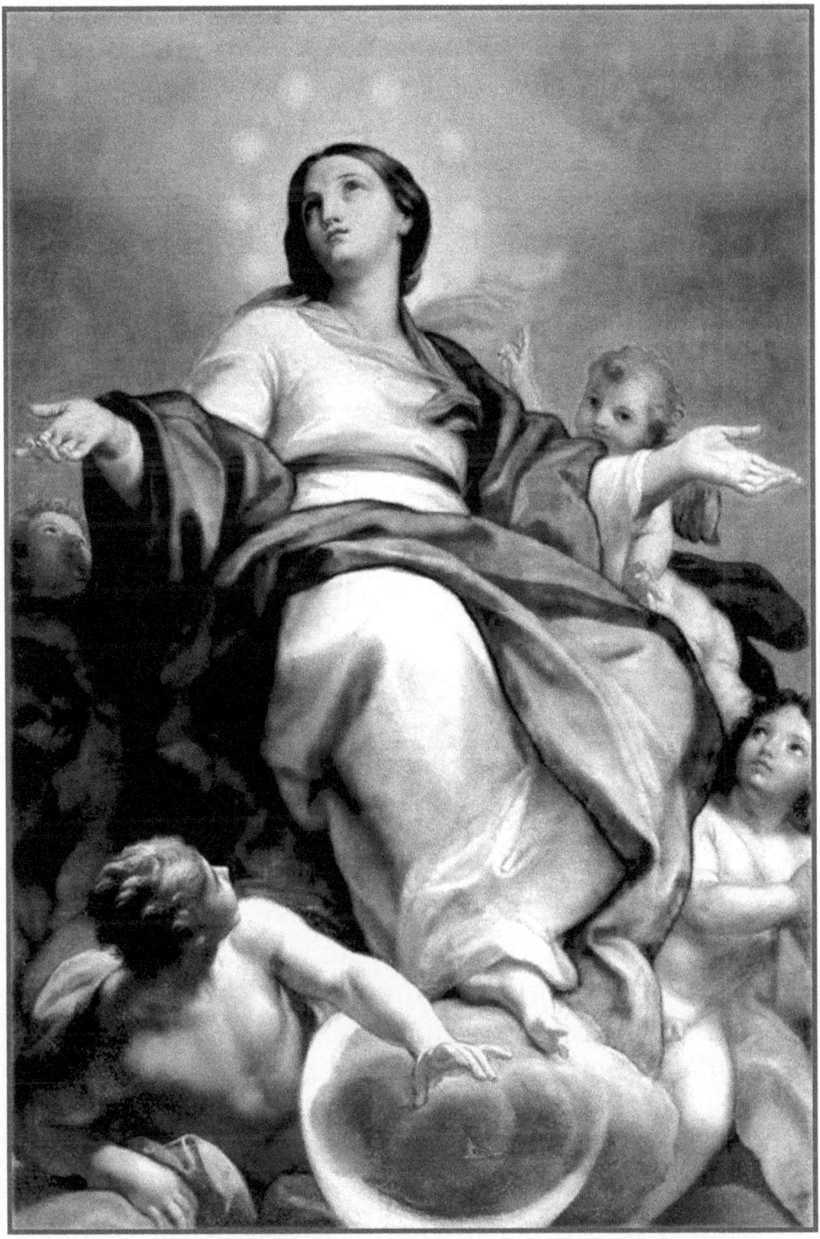

given to the messenger angel of the Incarnation; then to Elizabeth, who first proclaimed the Divine Maternity of Mary.

The second part, composed by the Church, expresses the most important prayer that we can formulate. Two instances are decisive for us: the present moment, to which an eternity responds, the *nunc* (now) which alone is in our power; and the moment of death, the last hour of life in time and here below on which all eternity depends. The Church makes us invoke the help of Mary for this double moment: 'Holy Mary, Mother of God, pray for us poor sinners, *now,* and *at the hour of our death.*'

So recite the *Ave Maria* often, repeat it constantly; the Church spares no effort to engage us to repeat this salutation so glorious to Mary, so terrible to the demon, so salutary to us.

Hence the *Angelus*, which in certain countries is simply called the *Ave Maria*: hence the Chaplet or the Rosary, which is a continuous repetition of the *Ave Maria*.

The Angelus. Three times a day the bell reminds you of the whole of religion: (first) the Trinity of the Divine Persons, by this triple invitation and by the triple repetition of the *Ave Maria*; the Incarnation, by the words that contain the narrative of this mystery; (second) the birth, death and the resurrection of Jesus Christ, in other words the Joyful, the Sorrowful and the Glorious mysteries, summarized in the prayer which concludes; finally the humility and obedience of Mary so well expressed by her reply to the heavenly messenger: 'Behold the handmaid of the Lord; let it be done to me according to thy word'; and her elevation to the dignity of Mother of God, recalled by these words: 'and the Word was made flesh and dwelt amongst us.'

– This practice was instituted to implore the help of Mary against the infidels. In our days the Church is attacked by a legion of unbelievers more dangerous, more relentless, more fatal than were the Mussulmans (Muslims) and other barbarians; the *Angelus* has therefore lost none of its opportunity.

The Kings and the Doctors

Around the year 910, Paris and the surrounding areas were devastated by a plague that was called the 'mal des ardents'.[24] All those who were able to take refuge in Notre Dame de Paris were saved. Hugues-le-Grand fed them there at his own expense.

King Robert the Pious erected in the palace an oratory dedicated to Mary, which was enlarged and transformed by St. Louis IX and became Sainte-Chapelle.

In the abbey of Saint-Victor located on the left bank of the Seine, there was an underground chapel dedicated to Notre Dame de Bonne-Nouvelle. It was

---

[24] The 'mal des ardents' or the 'Burning Sickness', was also given different names during the medieval period, the 'sacred fire', 'Saint-André 's fire', 'Saint-Marcel's fire', 'Saint-Antoine's fire', 'Hell fire'. It was a sickness caused by ergotism, a toxic condition produced by eating grain or grain products such as rye bread, or even grasses, infected with the ergot fungus. According to an account from 1089 AD, those who had this sickness, had "their entrails devoured by the ardor of the sacred fire, with ravaged limbs blackening like coals, which either died miserably, or retained life seeing their gangrenous feet and hands separate from the rest of the body, but many suffered from a contraction of the limbs which deformed them ." (Source, "L'Histoire", monthly N°74 dated January 1985.)

there that the monk Adam de Saint-Victor, a famous Latin poet of the Middle Ages, loved to sing the praises of Mary. One day he was composing a prose there which begins with these words: 'Salve Mater Salvatoris'. Suddenly, seized with a pious transport he exclaimed:

>*Salve, mater pietatis*
>*Et totius Trinitatis*
>*Nobile triclinium,*
>*Verbi tamen incarnati*
>*Specilae majestati*
>*Praeparans hospitium.*

>"Hail, Mother of piety
>And providing for the whole Trinity
>A noble room with three couches!
>But, for the majesty
>Of the Word incarnate,
>Preparing a special welcome!"

Immediately the crypt lit up and Mary appeared, bowing her head as if she wanted to approve the poet and thank him.

However, the ancient church of which Clovis had laid the first stone in the city seemed worthy neither of Mary nor of the capital. Thanks to his talents and his merit, Maurice de Sully, so named from the place of his origin, had become bishop of Paris despite the obscurity of his birth. He undertook to rebuild the basilica of Notre Dame de Paris. Louis-le-Jeune and the kings his successors, Philippe-Auguste, Louis VIII, St. Louis IX and Philippe III greatly assisted in this construction.

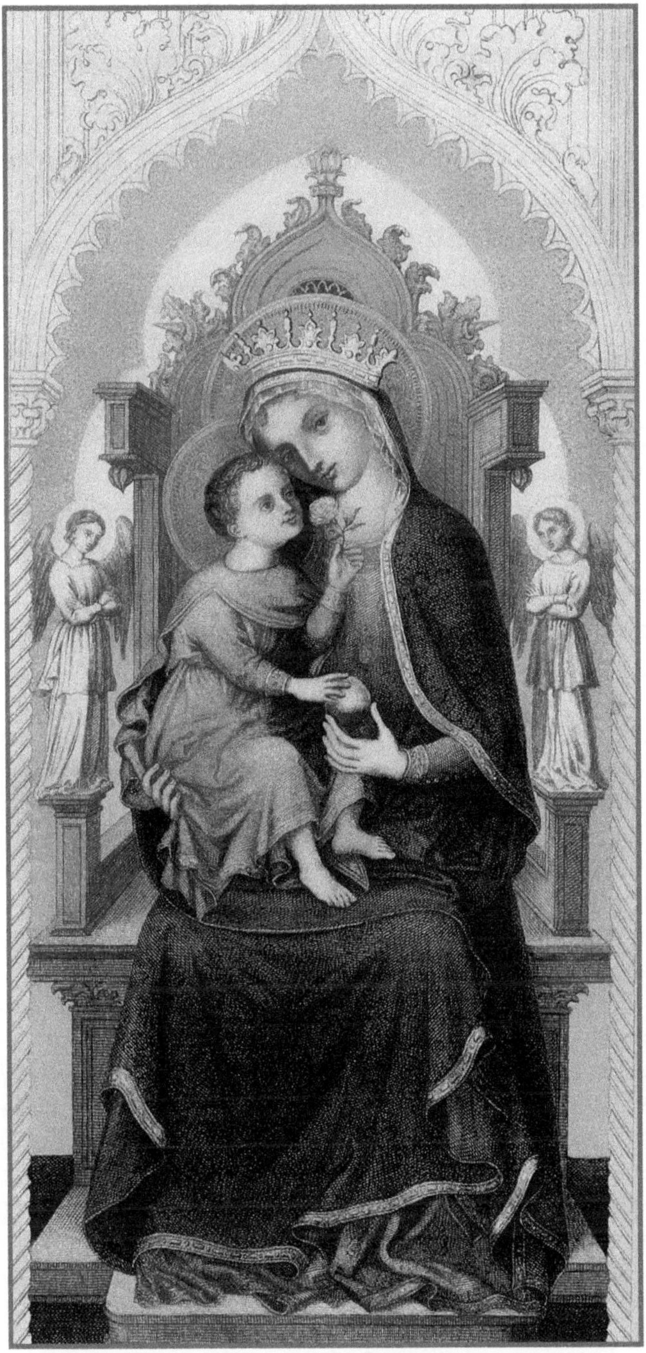

Louis-le-Jeune had been brought up in the cloister of Notre Dame, so he considered Mary as his mother.

In 1248, St. Louis IX built Sainte-Chapelle to place the Crown of Thorns there. But the lower part remained consecrated to Mary.

In 1304 the theological doctors of the Sorbonne had gathered to discuss the Immaculate Conception of Mary. The famous Duns Scotus on his way to the meeting, stopped in front of a statue of Our Lady which stood in the middle of the entrance courtyard: "Holy Virgin," he said, "grant that I praise you with dignity and confound your enemies." The statue bowed. Duns Scotus spoke so well that on that very day, the University of Paris decreed that henceforth no one was to be received as a doctor if he did not swear to support the privilege of the Immaculate Conception of Mary. [25]

---

[25] Bl. Duns Scotus, (c. 1265-1308), a Doctor of the Church and known as the 'Subtle Doctor', was given the grace to answer the two questions which had challenged theologians up to then and for which they could find no adequate explanation regarding her Immaculate Conception: first, if Mary required redemption if she had been conceived without the stain of original sin, and second, when exactly was it in the course of her conception she was preserved from the stain and effects of original sin.

Bl. Duns Scotus explained that she was indeed redeemed, Mary called God her Saviour in the Magnificat, but she had obtained the greatest of redemptions through the mystery of her preservation from all sin. This pre-redemption indicates a much greater grace and more perfect salvation, and attributes to Christ a more exalted role as Redeemer, for redeeming grace which preserves from original sin is greater than that which purifies from sin already incurred. He further explained Christ was Mary's Redeemer more perfectly by preservative redemption in shielding her from original sin through anticipating and foreseeing the merits of His passion and death. In other words, the limits of time was not a factor: God Is the great Eternal I Am

Duns Scotus

and not bound by time, Christ, Son of God and Second Person of the Holy Trinity, applied the merits of His Passion to her at the moment of conception. With Mary, conception and sanctification were simultaneous, producing a twofold situation at the first moment of existence.

*Louis XIV in Notre-Dame de Paris
on January 30, 1687 at a Thanksgiving Service
after his Recovery from a Grave Illness.*

This same year 1304 reminds us of the victory of Mons-en-Puelle won on the 17th of August by Philippe-le-Bel. Elsewhere we have said that the victor paid homage to Our Lady of Chartres with the horse and arms which had served her on that famous day. We must add here that, according to the king's intention, the commemorative feast of this victory was celebrated in Paris on the 18th of August.

The 23rd of August 1328, Philippe de Valois won at Mont-Cassel, a victory which he also attributed to the intervention of Mary; so, on returning to the capital, he went straight to Notre Dame and entered there mounted on the same horse and wearing the same arms as on the day of the battle. He advanced like this to the crucifix and offered Mary all his war gear. He then made the pilgrimage to Chartres to renew there the testimony of his gratitude.

Then came the bad days. During the captivity of King Jean, the city of Paris made a vow to present every year to the church of Notre Dame a candle the length of which would equal the circumference of the surrounding walls. This offering was made until 1605. At that time the long rolled candle was replaced by a silver lamp in the shape of a ship, symbol of the city, and by a large candle.[26] Louis XIV added six lamps to that of Paris. The tribute of the candle lasted until 1789.

---

[26] The huge candle was first presented to Notre Dame on August 14th, 1437, (which had to be presented coiled like a rope), and the tradition continued, the candle growing in length as the size of the environs spread out as the city expanded, until it was deemed the limit for the length had been reached and it was replaced in 1605 by a donation of a silver ship as a candle holder. The ship is a symbol of Paris. The silver ship was destroyed during the Revolution. (Source: "Notre Dame de Paris: A Short History & Description of the Cathedral, With Some Account of the Churches Which Preceded It" by Charles Hiatt, 2022)

*The Virgin of the Rosary with
Saint Catherine of Alexandria and Saint Catherine of Sienna,
Luis Lagarto (1611)*

8 ~ The Chaplet or Rosary

It is through the Rosary that St. Dominic converted the Albigensians; it is through the Rosary that more than once the Church has obtained the triumph of its warriors over the most formidable enemies of those bearing the name of Christian. The Feast of the Rosary proves it. Let us use this weapon against the enemies of our souls, and victory will confirm our legitimate hopes.

This practise unites the two forms of prayer: vocal prayer and mental prayer.

The vocal prayers of the Rosary are the most beautiful, the most pious, the most simple and the most solemn, as well as the most authoritative in religion. The profession of faith or the Apostles Creed opens the series. Then the Lord's Prayer, repeated several times in the course of the Rosary. Then the Angelic Salutation, returning first three times, after a first Pater, to honour the Holy Trinity, then repeating itself ten times after each of the 5 Paters, and finally the majestic Gloria Patri, ending each decade.

All these numbers offer a symbol. Three recalls the Three Divine Persons; ten figures the Ten Commandments of the Decalogue, and therefore the perfection of the Christian life. Five expresses the fingers of the hand, the organ of action. Fifty, complement of forty-nine, which is the product of seven multiplied by itself, recalls and the jubilee of the old law, and the Jewish and Christian Pentecost and the multiplication of the seven days of the week by themselves, multiplication of the merits amassed by the good use of the time of this present life, which must bring about the rest and the jubilee of the Eternal Day represented by the fiftieth jubilee year of the people of God.

There is not one passing from one bead to another that does not have its significance. The hand, organ of action and will, is united in this pious exercise with the tongue, the organ of thought and intelligence, and at the same time through meditation the mind passes over the principal mysteries of the hidden, suffering and glorious life of Jesus Christ. The Rosary is therefore, in every way, a complete course in religion.

To these practices no less solid than pious add:

The special celebration of Saturday, the day consecrated to Mary.

Recite, from time to time at least, the Little Office of the Blessed Virgin as a preparation for the most solemn feasts, such as the Immaculate Conception, the Nativity, the Annunciation, the Purification, and the Assumption.

Make pilgrimages to famous shrines; finally, there is the beautiful and joyful devotion of the Month of Mary.

You will feel your confidence and your devotion awakening, reviving, increasing ceaselessly, and after having lived with Mary, you will die invoking her, and you will go and share her joys and glories.

The Protestants and the Blessed Virgin of Paris

Formerly in Paris, every street corner was adorned with a gathering of flowers in the middle of which stood a small statue of the Blessed Virgin. On Saturdays, the niche was fully illuminated, and every night a lighted lamp shone at the foot of the statue. It was like the first street lighting. This pious custom was, moreover, common to most towns in France.

One of the first acts by which Protestantism made its presence known in Paris was through (its followers) mutilating and decapitating a statue of the Blessed Virgin placed at the corner of the Rue des Rosiers near the little Porte Saint-Antoine (in 1528).[27]

---

27   This was a historical event. It was one of the first cases of major sacrilegious vandalism against a public sacred image that 'co-incidentally' happened with the appearance of the Huguenots, who were Protestants. The body had been pierced, and the head-dress trampled under foot. The heads of the mother and child had been broken off and thrown into the trash heap. An outrageous act of contempt for the Catholic piety of the country, for the deed caused a huge scandal. The king offered a reward of a thousand crowns to find the culprits, but they were never found. A rumour circulated that a similar case of vandalism had been witnessed in a village about five leagues distant, and that the culprits had confessed they were prompted to do the deed by the promise of receiving one hundred *sous* as a reward for every sacred image they destroyed. There is no report they were punished, so it 'might' have been a fabrication: my source says it is not unlikely someone had done the deed and circulated the rumours to pin it on the Protestants in an act of persecution, (Source: "Ch. IV, Insult to an Image and an Expiatory Procession", in "History of the Rise of the Huguenots", by Henry M. Baird). But, we note it is highly

Francis I immediately ordered the making of a silver statue similar to the one that had been desecrated. Then he summoned all the ecclesiastical bodies of Paris to a church near the place of desecration together with eight bishops, the parliament, the chamber of accounts and the body of the city, the princes of the blood, the ambassadors and all the great officers of the Crown. The Holy Sacrifice was offered in expiation for the attack committed, and from there they went in procession to the scene of the crime, the grand chaplain of France carrying the new statue, the king following him with a candle in his hand. Arriving at the designated place, the bishop placed the statue on a prepared altar; the band of the royal chapel sang the antiphon '*Ave, Regina caelorum*' in front of the whole assembly on its knees; after which the king rose, and taking the statue, respectfully kissed it, placed it himself in the niche, closed the trellis intended to prevent new insults from happening, got back down on his knees, prayed for some time in tears, and with great pomp had the original mutilated statue taken to the Church of Saint-Gervais, where it has since

---

unlikely the pious people would do such a thing against their own sacred images, even in retaliation against the rise of the Huguenot Protestantism with the purpose of sparking a persecution against them. And, according to my source, there was a sudden increase of sacrilegious vandalism from this time onward with the rise of the Huguenots. The vandalism of public niche statues became so numerous that the government of Paris was at a loss of what to do and finally ordered two years later after the sacrilegious event of 1528 that any sacred representation placed on the exterior walls of a house could not be lower than ten feet off the ground so to prevent anyone reaching them. Considering Protestantism was making rapid inroads in Paris at the time, it is not unlikely some of its followers were causing the vandalism.

been honoured for centuries under the title Our Lady of Tolerance.

This title did not move the sectarians; in 1547 they broke the gate and stole the rich statue. It was replaced by a wooden statue, and in 1551 they also broke it. They, who demanded tolerance for their worship, were the most intolerant of men for the worship of the whole nation." (Source: Hamon).

The heresy however was making frightening progress. Parisians wishing to protect themselves from the scourge addressed Mary.

In 1529, an immense procession left Notre Dame de Paris and went to Notre-Dame des Vertus in Aubervillers, between Saint-Denis and the capital. All the parishes of Paris were united in this great demonstration. Each faithful carried a lighted torch and such was the brilliance of these innumerable lights that from the heights of Montlhéry it was believed that Paris was on fire.

Mary would answer these prayers, for from Paris would come forth the extraordinary help prepared by Heaven against the great heresy.

☙ ❀ ❧

9 ~ Mary in the Divine Plan

When an architect meditates on the plan of a building, a palace for example, or a temple, the first object of his thought, if it is a palace it will be the throne, and if it is a temple it will be the altar. In the second rank but before all the rest, comes the throne room for the palace, and for the temple it is the sanctuary. Then the artist traces the plan of the whole building, relating all the parts of the palace to the throne room, and thus to the throne itself and to the king, all the parts of the temple to the sanctuary, and thus to the altar and to God.

Thus, from all eternity, the Supreme Artist decides on the plan of a palace and a temple of which He is both the King and God. The throne in this palace, the altar in this temple is God made man, Jesus Christ. Also, whether by virtue of the anticipation of original sin or independently of this fall, the Incarnation being the highest outward manifestation of the grace of God, it may be said to be the primary object, the principle, the centre, the final end of the Divine Plan.

In the Eternal Decrees it was fixed that the God-Man would be born of a daughter of Adam, and that this daughter chosen above all would be the Virgin Mary. Therefore in the palace, in the temple of Creation where angels and men are the living stones of the edifice, Mary is like the throne room or the sanctuary, and through her everything from the tiny atom to the seraphim relates to Jesus Christ, Who alone, by His humanity, is the Throne of Supreme

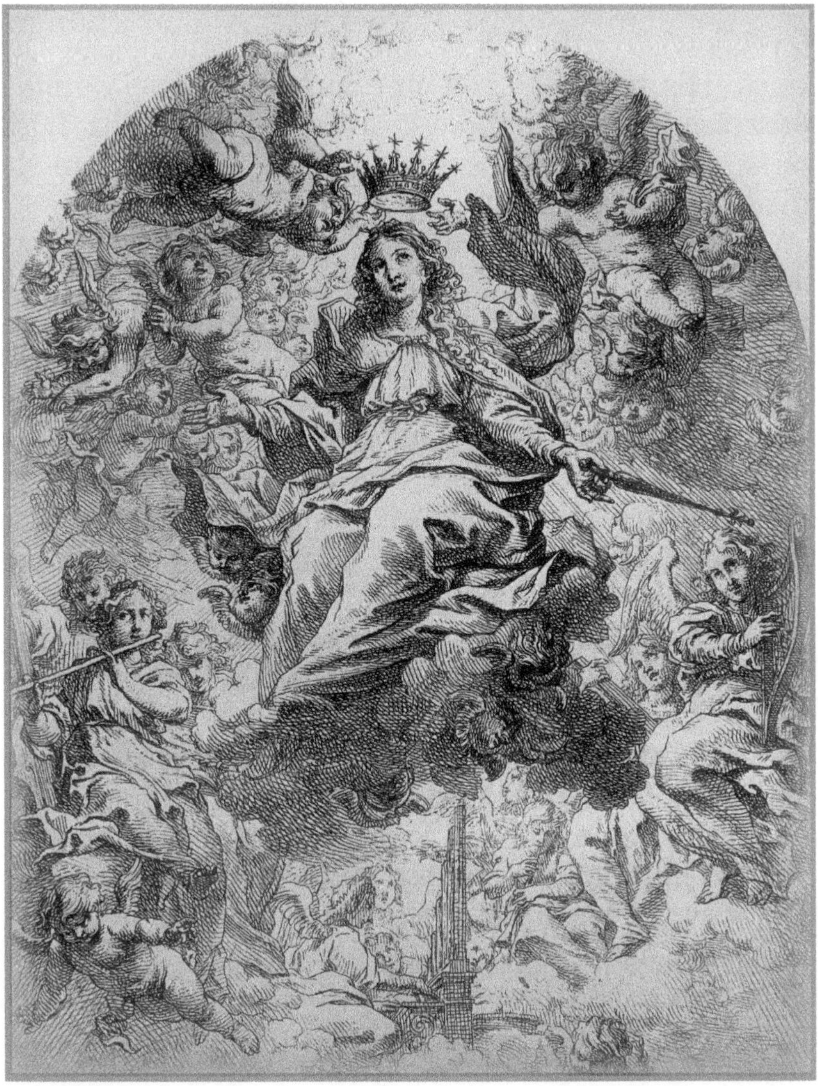

Royalty, the Altar of the Thrice-Holy Divinity. Such is the place that Mary occupies in the Eternal Plan of Creation, the first after her Divine Son. With Him she can say again: 'The Lord possessed me in His foreknowledge, in His decree at the beginning of His ways, His thoughts, His eternal purposes.' *Dominus possessed me in initio viarum suarum.* ("The Lord possessed me in the beginning of His ways, before He made any thing from the beginning," Proverbs 8:22)

Let us conclude with St. Anselm: "All that exists is above or below Mary; God alone is above, all mere creatures below;" and with St. Bonaventure, "God can create a larger world, a heaven higher than the world and heavens that exist, but He cannot raise a mere creature higher than that which He has made His Mother." For, as Albert the Great declares, "The dignity of the Mother of God comes immediately after that of God Himself," and "Mary cannot be more united to God than she is, unless she becomes God." (Id.) Also, "Such is the greatness of Mary," according to St. Bernardine, "that only God can understand her."

Everything in the world relates to Jesus Christ; everything is an announcement of Jesus Christ. Before His coming, everything prepares for Him and figures Him; since His coming, everything is a continuation and an imitation of His life and action. In the same way everything in the world relates to Mary, either to announce her or to recall her.

Let us not forget that in this palace and in this temple we too have a marked place. By His humanity Jesus Christ is the throne of this palace, the altar of this temple; Mary is the throne room and sanctuary, and we are to form the rest of the building and be its living stones: *Superaedificati super fundamentum apostolorum* ("Built upon the foundation of the apostles and prophets," Eph. 2:20) *Quae domus sumus nos.* ("Of which house we are", Heb. 3:6)[28]

Let us take care. The stone that does not meet the architect's design is thrown back into the rubble. If there is in us any work, any word, any thought which does not conform to the required measure, which does not refer to God through Jesus, and to Jesus through Mary, this act is wrong; for then there is no place for him in this palace, in this temple which is called the Church here below, nor in heaven above. Such is the law. From the first *fiat*, (let there be) from *fiat lux*, (be light made) to *fiat mihi secundum verbum tuum*, (be it done to me according to thy word), from Creation to the Last Judgement, everything in the world as well as in man, everything in the public life of nations as well in the private life of individuals, everything must relate to God through Jesus Christ and to Jesus Christ through Mary.

Thus the Old Testament is the continuous announcement of Mary. It would take a volume to show all the texts that can relate to the Mother of He Who is the Principle, the Centre and the End of all things. We will indicate some of them.

St. Ignatius ~ St. Francis de Sales

On the side of the hill of Montmartre there once existed a church under the name of Sainte-Marie and Saint-Denis. On the day of the Assumption 1534, seven

---

28   "But Christ as the Son in his own house: which house are we, if we hold fast the confidence and glory of hope unto the end." (Heb. 3:6)

young men belonging to various nations yet who were all students of the University of Paris, met in the crypt of this sanctuary. One of them, the only one who was a priest, celebrated the Holy Mass. At the time of Communion all of them committed themselves by vow to the service of God and to the defence of the Church. The leader of this new militia was called Ignatius de Loyola. The Company of Jesus (Jesuits) had just been born in Paris on the Mount of Martyrs, in a sanctuary of Mary, and on the day of one of her greatest feasts.[29]

In Saint-Étienne des Grès, a statue of the Blessed Virgin under the title of Notre-Dame de Bonne Délivrance was venerated there.[30] A young student

---

[29] Unfortunately the original crypt chapel where the vow was made was destroyed during the Revolution. The current crypt is located on the perimeter of the parish of Saint-Pierre de Montmartre. It was built between 1884 and 1887 in the chapel of the Society of the Helpers of the Holy Souls (Sœurs Auxiliatrices du Purgatoire), a female religious congregation taking inspiration from Ignatius, founded in the nineteenth century by Bl. Eugénie Smet (1825-1871).

[30] Saint-Étienne-des-Grès was located on the Rue Saint-Jacques, which is now the present Faculty of Law. The church had contained a Black Madonna statue called *Notre Dame de Bonne Délivrance* (Our Lady of Good Deliverance), also known as the Black Madonna of Paris. The Royal Confraternity of Notre Dame de Bonne Délivrance was established in 1533. Louis XIII and Anne of Austria were members. The shine was visited by many notable French saints, such as St. Vincent de Paul, and it was before this statue that St. Francis de Sales was inspired to pick up the prayer tablet and prayed to Our Lady the 'Memorare'. He was delivered from the obsessive temptation that he was already damned. When the collegiate church was demolished in 1792 during the Revolution, its contents were sold, but the statue was saved by a pious woman who later donated it to the Sisters of St. Thomas of Villeneuve. The statue is located in the chapel of the Congregation of the Sisters of St. Thomas of Villeneuve, 52 Blvd. d'Argenson, Neuilly-sur-Seine, outside of

often came to pray before this image. His name was Francis de Sales and he was only seventeen at the time. (1578) For several weeks he had been visibly wasting away; he could no longer drink, eat or sleep. In the grip of a frightful despair, he thought himself already damned. One day when prostrated at the feet of Our Lady of Good Deliverance he prayed with more earnestness and exclaimed: "Good Mother, if I am condemned to hate God for eternity, at least grant me to serve Him and to love Him during this life." Then he took a vow of chastity and undertook, in memory of this vow, to recite every day a rosary of six decades.[31] Instantly he was delivered and with peace of soul he recovered health in body.

ಐ☙ಐ

Paris. The feast of Our Lady of Good Deliverance is July 18.

[31] Of interest, the locals of Lourdes used to pray the six decade rosary. Our Lady of Lourdes appeared with a six decade rosary. With the extra decade, St. Bernadette would honour the Immaculate Conception as the first mystery in the Joyful mysteries, the Pietà as the sixth mystery in the Sorrowful mysteries, and Our Lady as Mediatrix of all graces as the sixth Glorious mystery.

10 ~ The Terrestrial Paradise

(Genesis 2: 8-15)

This radiant garden of paradise which God Himself had planted symbolises Mary formed by God with special care.

The unique river that divides into the four rivers that water the garden, this recalls the grace with which the Lord filled her heart with the fundamental virtues of the moral order. Who would not admire the lofty prudence of her thoughts, the justice of her will, the heroic strength with which she stands before the cross, and the inviolable purity of her heart?

By the grace of their foliage, by the brightness of their flowers, by the sweetness of their fruits, the trees of paradise announce the holy desires, the sweet words and the fruitful works of which the life of the faithful Virgin would be composed.

The docility of the animals to the voice of man then innocent represents the empire that the Immaculate Virgin always retained over her senses and her passions.

The first Adam was to guard paradise by cultivating it. The Second and True Adam will be able to guard the paradise that must receive Him on earth. First, He preserves the one who will be His Mother from all the attacks of the serpent and from all sin. Then for thirty years His sole occupation, it seems, will be to cultivate this already beautiful garden and to develop all the virtues there.

Creation of the World and the Garden of Eden

It is up to us to transform our soul into a spiritual paradise. Grace spreads there symbolised by the four rivers, grace for the intelligence through the four Gospels, and grace for the will through the four cardinal virtues. Fertilized by the teachings of faith and by the outpourings of charity, the soul will produce all the virtues, from the most modest represented by the flowering grass with which the hills of paradise are covered, to the great and sublime heroisms represented by the majesty of the cedar and by the strength of the oak. Faith also and charity will submit our senses and our passions to reason and to the will, as the animals were (submissive) to man in Eden.

But let us know how to guard and cultivate this paradise of our soul. By exercise and practice will we develop in our hearts the virtues, the seed of which was planted there through baptism and Holy Communion. Let us guard Jesus in our hearts and Jesus will guard us like He guarded Mary.

The Vow of Louis XIII

After the death of Henry IV the Protestants rose up on all sides. It was to the assistance of Mary that Louis XIII attributed his victories, and especially the recapture of La Rochelle, stronghold of the heresy and of the revolt. To recognize this powerful intervention, on the 9th of December 1629 the young king laid the first stone of Notre-Dame des Victoires, today so famous by the Archconfraternity of the Immaculate Heart of Mary. After the birth of Louis XIV, his mother Anne of Austria had the chapel of the Blessed Virgin decorated, which can be found in this church.

But here is a more solemn act. It was the 10th of February 1638. Louis XIII, in full grand dress, entered the church of Notre Dame de Paris. He carried the sceptre and the crown to place both at the feet of the image of Mary. An edict explains the scope of this imposing ceremony. In the letters patent he published that very day, the king listed first the favours he has received from Heaven since the beginning of his reign:

> "The rebellion of heresy abated; the arms of France always victorious, and the leagues which his enemies had formed against him struck with impotence.
>
> "By all these reasons, prostrating ourselves," says Louis XIII, "at the feet of the Divine Majesty Whom we adore in Three Persons, and at those of the Blessed Virgin and of the sacred cross where we revere the accomplishment of the mysteries of our redemption by the life and death of the Son of God in our flesh, we believe ourselves obliged to consecrate ourselves to the greatness of God by His Son, brought down to us, and to this Son by His Mother, raised up to Him, under the protection of which we very specially wish to place ourselves in order to obtain, by her intercession, under the protection of the Blessed Trinity, and by her authority and example, the protection of the whole celestial court. Accordingly, we hereby declare that, taking the Most Blessed and

Most Glorious Virgin as our special protector of our realm, we particularly consecrate our person, our state, our crown, and our subjects to her; begging her to inspire us with such a holy conduct and to maintain this kingdom with so much care, that whether in peace or at war, there will be nothing but those paths of grace that lead to those of glory, and so that the memory of this consecration remains forever in posterity, we order that there be made every year, on the day of the Assumption, after vespers, in all the churches, cathedrals, parishes or concentuelles of our States, a very solemn procession where all the judicial and civil authorities will attend. Our intention is that the bishops recommend to all our people to have a special devotion towards the Blessed Virgin, and to implore, on this solemn day, her protection over France, so that, under such a powerful Patroness, our kingdom may be protected from all the enterprises of our enemies, may it enjoy a long peace, and may God be served and revered there so perfectly, that we and our subjects may come to the blessed end for which we were created."

"This edict was put into execution the following 15th of August, and on the 5th of September after a sterility of twenty-two years, the queen gave birth to a child who was Louis XIV; and from this eminently national wish sprang the great century; for it is a remarkable thing that the fine geniuses who then carried so high, in all genres, the glory of the human spirit, almost all had a religious character: Bossuet and Corneille who walk at their head, were one and the other the humblest servants of Mary.

"Louis XIV, worthy to be the king of such subjects, faithfully renewed every year the consecration made by his father, and he did it with a heart frankly disposed towards Mary, for every day he recited the rosary in her honour; and one day when Father de la Rue, his confessor, had surprised him in this pious exercise, he said to him: "Don't be so surprised, Father; I hold this practice of the queen my mother; I take pride in it and I would be sorry to miss a single day."

"The secular year after the issuance of the vow of Louis XIII, Louis XIV solemnly renewed it and up to the present day when this vow is still fulfilled each year, if we except the disastrous period when the cult of the true God was forbidden in our temples, France has never ceased to revere in Mary her glorious patroness; as Mary has never ceased to protect us, snatching this kingdom from the most dreadful storms, and from the depths of the abyss where several times it has been believed to be swallowed up, always causing it to arise and reappear on the horizon the first kingdom of world." (Quote from Hamon, *Our Lady of France)*

However reason 'deified' under the living symbol of an infamous prostitute (during the Revolution), dared to show herself on the altar of Notre Dame in place of the statue of the Immaculate Virgin![32] Is it still permissible to say that France is the kingdom of Mary? Is it not to be feared that Mary will finally abandon Paris to her impieties and her iniquities?

No, Mary has since given in Paris itself new pledges of her protection, and these pledges surpass all that she had done until then to show her maternal solicitude.

༄༅༈༄༅

11 ~ The Tree of Life

(Genesis 2:9)

In the middle of paradise rose the Tree of Life; within Mary rises the Tree of Life, Jesus. Or better yet, the Church is paradise, Mary is the tree that bears and gives to the world the Fruit of Life: *benedictus fructus*

---

[32] The Revolutionaries desecrated Notre Dame, 're-dedicating' it as the 'temple of Reason' to the 'cult of the Supreme Being', a heretical Deist concept of God, and some sources say they sacrilegiously dared to enthrone a prostitute on the high altar, whom they declared to be 'the goddess of reason'. Others say it was the wife of a printer whom they 'enthroned' under this title. No matter who was enthroned, it was a horrific desecration.

ventris tui, Jesus: (*Blessed is the fruit of thy womb, Jesus.*) Jesus, the Bread descended from heaven, living Bread, the Bread of Life, life of the intelligence by His word which is light and truth, life of the will by His grace which is fire, justice and charity. Without Jesus and without His doctrine, the truth, even with reason which, moreover, is insufficient because of our elevation to the supernatural order, the truth becomes altered. (Without Him and His doctrine), truth deteriorates and soon vanishes in the darkness of lies and of errors. Without Jesus, without Christian justice and charity, the moral virtue, which is true freedom, disappears to make way for the brutal servility of passion and the cowardly terrors of human respect.

Mary is still the Ark of Life in the sense that throughout the duration of her existence there is not one action, not one word, not one thought which is not a fruit of life, a fruit of grace, a fruit of glory. Grace is their principle and communicates to them a supernatural life; glory is the term and assures them of eternal life.

In the fruit of the plant God deposited a seed which contains in its germ a series of plants which can follow one another without end. This germ is therefore the principle of a life which could be prolonged eternally. Likewise, in the acts that we produce under the influence of grace, there is the seed of another grace which, in turn contains another, and so on, until finally the last grace becomes for us eternal glory. Who can grant us, as was granted to Mary, (the grace) not to produce an action, not to utter a word, not to conceive a thought, not to have a desire unless animated by grace and worthy of glory, (or do anything) that is not a fruit of supernatural life and thus a fruit of eternal life?

Let us unite our heart through the heart of Mary to the Heart of Jesus. The heart is the principle of movement and therefore of life. May the Heart of Jesus through the Heart of Mary be the first motive of our heart, may it be the principle and the end of all its movements, and then everything in us will be life: grace in time and glory in eternity.

The Miraculous Medal

In 1830, on the 8th of December, a daughter of St. Vincent de Paul was praying in the chapel of the Mother House, Rue du Bac. She thought of the misfortunes of the times. Suddenly she heard a rustle of wings. A light both bright and soft struck her eyes. Rays shone from the left side of the altar. There, in the midst of the light, appears a noble and beautiful Lady, her feet resting on a globe, her arms lowered towards the ground, her hands open and letting jets of light escape, her head bent slightly forward as if to listen. A crown of stars shone on her forehead. Then an angel said to the sister: "Recognize the Queen of the Heaven. The rays that come from her hands represent the graces that she spreads over men. Then a caption surrounded Mary herself, and the sister read these words: "O Mary conceived without sin, pray for us who have recourse to thee." She also saw an M surmounted by a cross, and below the M two hearts, one pierced and also surmounted by a cross, the other pierced by a sword. They were the Hearts of Jesus and Mary. Twelve stars surrounded this symbolic set.

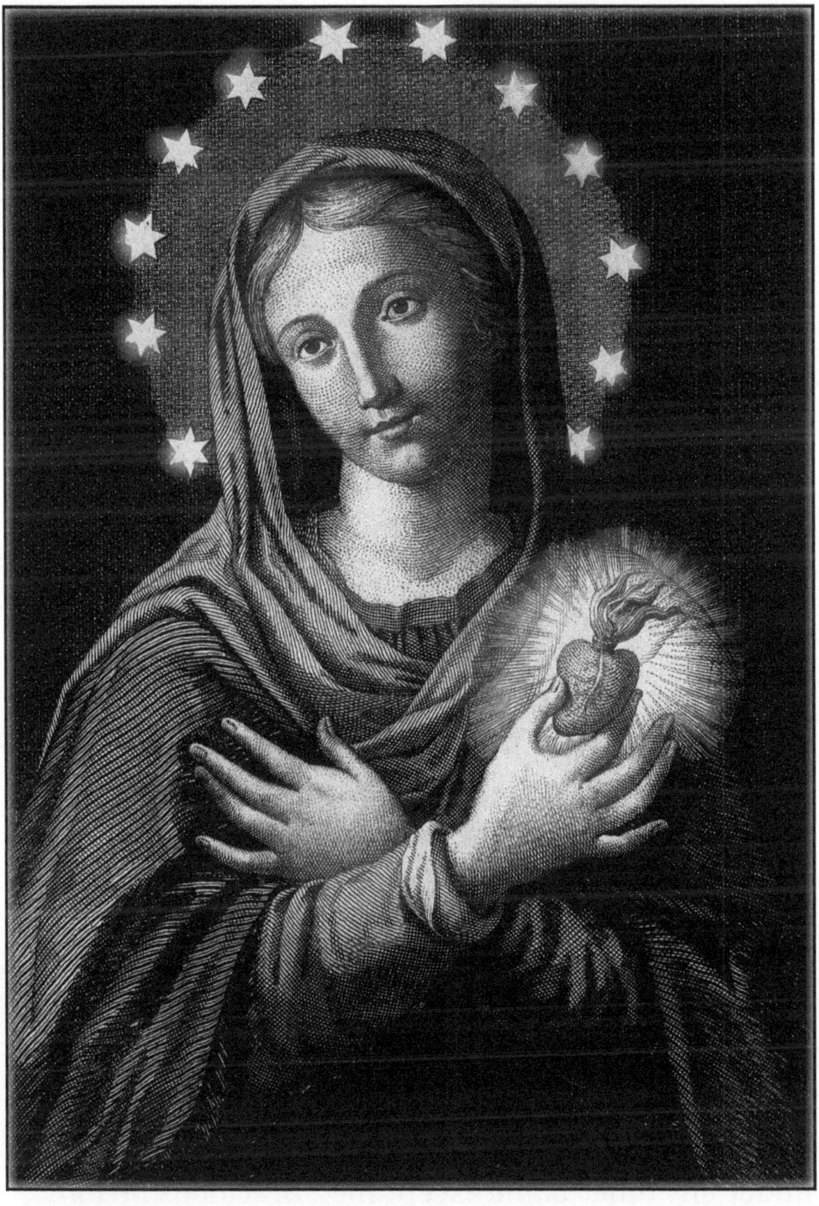

The angelic voice resumed in these terms: "Servant of God and of the poor, beloved daughter of Mary, your charity and your piety have made you find favour in her eyes. She orders you to strike a medal representing what you have seen. This medal being indulged will be like a shield for those who wear it and who will say: "O Mary conceived without sin, pray for us who have recourse to thee." The angel fell silent and the vision disappeared. The medal was struck and thanks to its origin, thanks above all to the prodigies of protection for the body and conversion for the soul which took place by its presence, it is no longer known under any other name except the Miraculous Medal.

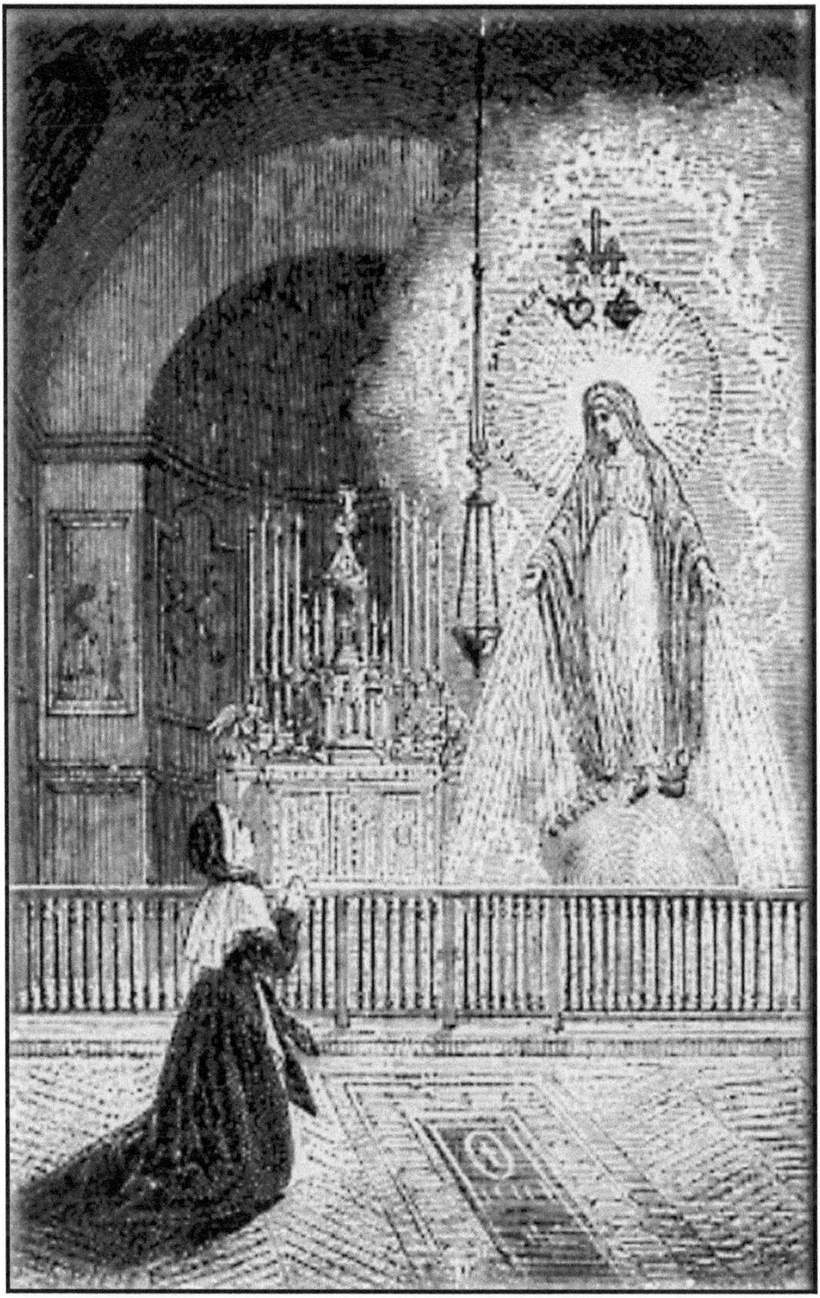

12 ~ Noah's Ark

(Genesis 7: 12-22)

All flesh had corrupted its ways, God would obliterate mankind: but He has encountered a just man. On the Divine order this just one will work a hundred years on the construction of the ark that by bearing him must also save the human race.

A hundred years form a century, and if the century represents the universality of time, it also represents eternity. From time immemorial and from all eternity, the true Noah, the One who will be the 'Second Father' of the human race because He will be its Saviour, Jesus Christ prepares in the person of Mary this Ark of Salvation which would bear Him, He Who would save the world.

The ark escapes the fury of the floods of the Deluge because of the righteous it carries within; Mary will be preserved from original sin, because of the One she must carry in her womb.

Like Mary, be the ark of the true Noah. Receive Jesus and carry Him within yourself. Jesus is the Truth: by faith keep His word in your understanding; you will escape the deluge of those errors which under the false name of ideas and principles dominate and submerge the highest mountains, the proudest intelligences, the powerful and famous men of the age. Jesus is justice: by charity keep His grace in your heart, and you will escape the deluge of those vices which cover and engulf the highest mountains, the giants of the age.

Do you see these powerful and famous men, do you see them as they roll, uplifted here by the rising tide of senseless pride, there dragged down into the abyss of voluptuousness? Seized and swept away in the whirlwinds of vice, they disappear one after the other, swallowed up forever, they, their works and their memory. *Isti sunt potentes a saeculo viri famosi ...* ("these are the mighty men of old, men of renown", Gen. 6:4)[33] Yesterday, we named them with

---

33   The 'mighty men of renown' or giants were destroyed during the Flood. The Douay-Rheims Bible notes they as being not only tall in stature, "but violent and savage in their dispositions, and mere monsters of cruelty and lust." Here,

trembling! Today, what remains of their high deeds? Nothing.

Finally understand that on the day of the Flood there is no salvation except in the ark, in the Church of Jesus Christ, in the Heart of Mary, Mother of Jesus Christ, in the very Heart of Jesus Christ.

Notre Dame des Victoires

In 1836, Mary intervened in another way in the very centre of Paris. Not far from the Stock Exchange in a quarter where no other devotion was known other than that of gold, stood an almost deserted church. It was Notre Dame des Victories (Our Lady of Victories) whose glorious origin we have recalled. One day the venerable parish priest of this church, the Abbé Desgenettes, felt urged to establish a prayer association in honour of the Immaculate Heart of Mary for the conversion of sinners. "What," he replied to the interior call, "a confraternity, a devotion for parishioners who do not even come to Mass on Sundays!" Unable, however, to drive away this thought which constantly obsessed him, one Sunday the good priest announced to the small number of faithful present at Mass that in the evening after vespers he would receive the names of the people who wanted to enlist in a confraternity in honour of the Immaculate Heart of Mary. He hardly counted on a few pious

---

Fr. de Boylesve shows they represent the 'giants' of our times, the great men of the world and their sinful ways and passions, their works and vice-ridden lifestyles may seem great in the eyes of the world but not to God, they will be swept away like the giants of old and their works.

women. What was his surprise in the evening when he had registered more than four hundred names! Now, today, who will say the number of miracles wrought in favour of those who have been recommended to the prayers of the Archconfraternity of Our Lady of Victories? Who can count the names inscribed on the registers of the innumerable members affiliated with this marvellous association?

Another favour to which Mary will show herself not to be a stranger was granted in a sanctuary in Paris. It was July 26, 1846. A sister of St. Vincent de Paul was praying in her community oratory. Jesus appeared to her holding in His right hand a scarlet scapular whose cords were of wool and of the same colour. On one part of this scapular was represented the crucified Saviour; at the foot of the cross there were the instruments of the Passion. Around it were these words: "Holy Passion of Jesus Christ our Saviour, save us." On the other part was the image of the Sacred Hearts of Jesus and Mary, a cross seemed to pierce them both at once. Around it this invocation read: "Sacred Hearts of Jesus and Mary, protect us."

This apparition repeated itself several times. Finally, on the day of the Exaltation of the Holy Cross, the sister heard these words: "Those who wear this scapular, will receive every Friday a great increase in faith, hope and charity." On June 25, 1847, Pius IX approved this devotion and enriched it with a large number of indulgences.[34]

---

34 See Appendix Three for more details on the Passion Scapular

This union of the Two Hearts and the Two Names of Jesus and Mary seems to us a new pledge of the intervention of the Virgin Mary and of the assistance she brings to the merciful designs of her Divine Son on the capital of France. This last favour also proves that neither France nor its capital are yet abandoned by Jesus and Mary. It is not at this hour, it is not at the time when true Catholics show themselves, in Paris itself, with so much courage, zeal and devotion, it is not yet the time to raise up the monument in honour of the Sacred Heart of Jesus for the repentance of guilty France,[35] it is not at this hour that one is allowed to despair. It is time to fight, it is time to suffer, maybe it is still time to die. Well! Today the fight, the suffering, the martyrdom: tomorrow the victory, the triumph and the salvation.

※

---

[35] I.e. the sanctuary that Christ asked for. One of the graces Christ promised would be the protection of France from its enemies if all the requests revealed to St. Margaret Mary were met, which included the construction of a shrine in honour of His Sacred Heart. The basilica of Sacre Coeur was started in 1875 to fulfil this request, and perhaps in its still incomplete state at the time Fr de Boylesve must have thought the promise of protection would not be kept until the work was finished. Little did he know that on the very day the cornerstone was consecrated, it was revealed to the mystic Marie-Julie Jahenny (1850-1941) that France was saved, the construction had commenced. Many of the chastisements threatening them at the time, such as the wars and the foretold destruction of Paris, were therefore postponed.

13 ~ **The Rainbow**

(Genesis 9: 12-17)

However, as in the dark days of the Flood, error and vice condense like vapours into thick clouds that intercept the light and heat of the sun of truth and justice. The lightning rumbles again, it will again burst on the guilty world. But suddenly the rainbow shone, and in the midst of this threatening night we saw sweet and brilliant Mary appear at La Salette, at Lourdes, at Pontmain. Immediately God remembered His promise: the world did not perish: *Apparebit arcus meus in nubibus, et recordabor foederis mei vobiscum.* ("My bow shall appear in the clouds, and I will remember My covenant with you, Gen. 9:14-15)

The rainbow results from the decomposition of the light ray which, penetrating into the cloud, is divided according to the laws of refraction, so as to spread out the seven colours which together constitute light.

The radiance of the Divine Sun of justice and truth would dazzle our eye. Passing through the heart of Mary, this bright light softens and offers itself to us in the varied form of the seven gifts of the Holy Spirit. Admire the Filial Awe of the Virgin on the Day of the Annunciation: her Maternal Piety as she seeks Jesus; the Knowledge that she stores in her heart by keeping there and comparing each of the words and actions of her Divine Son: *Conservabat omnia verba haec conferens in cord suo*: (" But Mary kept all these words, pondering them in her heart," Luke 2:9); her

Notre-Dame de la Garde at Marseilles

Strength when she stands near the cross; her docility to the Interior Counsel which made her prefer virginity to the very honour of Divine Maternity; Intelligence which makes her penetrate the mysteries of the Heart of her Son, and Wisdom which makes her appreciate and taste the sweetness hidden in the pains of the cross.

The seven colours of the rainbow can also represent the sacraments which together constitute the Church, which also constantly reminds God of the covenant He has contracted with the world.

The sacraments also contribute to producing in the faithful soul the grace which unites it to God and which, through the seven gifts of the Holy Spirit, makes it a rainbow in the supernatural order.

Holy Orders itself and the sacrament of Marriage exert their influence on those who do not receive them: the first gives the priest the power to confer grace, the second gives parents the grace to raise their children in a Christian way.

Mary at Marseilles

One day a vessel without oars and without sails was seen approaching near Marseilles. This vessel carried the friends of Jesus whose presence annoyed the Jewish deicides.

They had been placed on a ship without tackle and left to the mercy of the winds and waves. The breath of Providence pushed the exiles towards Gaul. Chief among them were Lazarus and his two sisters, Martha and Mary Magdalen. Mary Salomé, mother of the Apostles St. James and St. John. Mary, mother of the other James, Ruf, and also the sons of Simon the Cyrene, and Maximin and Nymphe his niece.

Barely landed, Lazarus erected on the shore an altar of earth in honour of the Mother of God who was yet living. A spring of living water gushed out at the foot of this modest monument. It was the symbol of the graces that were to flow to Gaul through the intercession of Mary. Lazarus then came to Marseilles with Magdalene. He preached the Gospel there and erected another altar where Notre-Dame de Confession is venerated.[36]

Near Marseilles rises a hill where a temple of Venus was once seen. In 1214, a pious person named Peter built a modest oratory there in honour of the Blessed Virgin. The influx of pilgrims made this sanctuary famous, under the name of Notre-Dame de la Garde. Sailors are very devoted to her. On their return from their travels, as soon as they see the chapel all manoeuvres cease, silence falls, the sailors fall to their knees and bare-headed they sing the *Salve Regina* in chorus. The kings of France who visited Marseilles made it their duty to climb the holy mountain. The men of '93 (Revolutionaries) closed the chapel. The silver statue was removed. But since then, the devotion of Notre Dame de la Garde has resumed its brilliance and the piety of the Marseillais has replaced the old oratory with a splendid church the inauguration of which took place on the 5th of June, 1864 in the presence of fifty bishops.

ಐ✵ಎ

---

[36] The statue of Our Lady here is depicted wearing a green dress, and it is tradition to touch green candles to the statue before lighting them. The main pilgrimage to this shrine takes place on Candlemas, February 2nd.

14 ~ Jacob's Ladder

(Genesis 28: 10-17)

Mary is Jacob's ladder. A child of Adam, like us she touches the earth. Mother of Jesus, she reaches for heaven. Her prayers and her holy desires ascend unceasingly to heaven; while Divine grace continues to descend from heaven into her heart. Through her the Son of God, the Word will descend to earth; through her, sons of Adam, poor sinners, we will ascend to heaven. Through Mary our prayer will ascend to the Heart of Jesus, through Mary the grace of Jesus will descend into our heart.

We too are represented by the mysterious ladder: by the body we touch the earth, by the soul we touch Heaven. If we want it, our works, our words, our desires, our thoughts will be as so many steps which will raise us to God. It depends on us to ascend unceasingly to God by prayer and contemplation, and to descend unceasingly to our neighbour by the action of zeal and charity. Then our life will be Jacob's ladder, and God will rest in us and over us.

Notre-Dame de Pignans (Diocese of Fréjus)[37]

Among the disciples of the Saviour who landed at Marseilles with Lazarus and his two sisters was St. Nymphe, the niece of St. Maximin, first Bishop of Aix.

---

[37] i.e. Notre-Dame-des-Anges de Pignans.

She built a chapel in honour of the Blessed Virgin on a height once occupied by a Roman camp which gave birth to the town of Pignans (*castra pinorum*). St. Nymphe suffered martyrdom in Marseilles at the same time as Lazarus. The oratory of Pignans was overthrown by the pagans. When peace had been restored to the Church by Constantine, a shepherd discovered an image of Mary hidden in the brush on the top of the mountain. Convinced that it was the statue venerated at the time of St. Nymphe, the Christians rebuilt the chapel. Later, King Thierry, one of the sons and successors of Clovis, restored the building, and in 508 AD he gave a charter where it is said that in this place an image of Mary carved on wood had been honoured from the time of the disciples of the Saviour.[38]

Notre Dame de Grâce at Cotignac (Diocese of Fréjus)

On the 10th of August 1519, a farmer named Jean de la Baume, in other words, de la Sacco, went during the morning to his work on the hill of Verdale. Suddenly the Mother of God appeared to him within a great light. She ordered him to inform the community of ecclesiastics established in Cotignac and the

---

[38] On the feast of the nativity of Our Lady, September 8, the faithful of the parish of Pignans make a procession to the sanctuary of Notre-Dame-des-Anges de Pignans situated at the top of the Massif des Maures. During this annual pilgrimage, the Virgin is adorned with flowers and the faithful receive blessed roses, a tradition which first started when King Thierry restored the shrine and has continued though the centuries.

notables of the city that she wanted to have a chapel on this hill where she would be invoked under the title of Notre Dame de Grâce. At first they refused to believe in the apparition, but a second apparition having taken place, the chapel was built and it was not long in becoming famous by the number of miracles and by the attendance of the pilgrims.

This sanctuary holds a special rank among those where Mary was invoked for the birth of Louis XIV. We will come back to this later.

Demolished in 1793, the chapel of Notre Dame de Grâce was rebuilt in 1810 and pilgrimages resumed their course.

Notre Dame d'Embrun (Diocese of Gap)

The sanctuary of Notre Dame d'Embrun goes back to St. Marcellin, apostle of the region, or at least to his immediate successor, Artémius. Destroyed by the barbarian invasions, it was rebuilt with magnificence by Charlemagne. People venerated there a painting called 'royal', or simply 'le Réal', or the Virgin du Réal, because it represented the Blessed Virgin and the Three Wise Men. Louis XI wore a medal of Notre Dame d'Embrun on his hat. He was appointed by Sixtus IV first canon of this church. Charles VIII, Louis XII, Francis I, Henry II came to pray at this sanctuary. In 1585, the Huguenots, under the leadership of Lesdiguières, ransacked it and destroyed the miraculous image of the Virgin du Réal. Henry IV returned the church to the Catholics. Louis XIII visited it in 1639.

Notre Dame du Laus (Diocese of Gap)

In the month of May 1664, a shepherdess named Benoît Reneurel was grazing her sheep on the mountain of Saint-Maurice. St. Maurice appeared to her and told her that the next day in the Saint-Étienne valley she would see a great Lady who later would reveal her name. The next day, the shepherdess went to the place indicated, and on a rock called Les Fours she saw a beautiful Lady with a small Child. After two months of frequent appearances, the Lady said: "I am Mary, Mother of Jesus, tell M. the Prior to come here in procession with his parish." The procession took place. Later a chapel was erected in this place, under the name of Notre Dame des Fours. This was at the end of August 1664.

A month later, Mary appeared to the shepherdess and ordered her to follow a path through a wood. Benoît obeyed and arrived at a chapel which had been built in 1640 by the inhabitants of Laus, but which was then quite dilapidated. Mary showed herself again and said to the shepherdess: "In a little while I will build a large church here, where many sinners will be converted. The poor will provide the money, and you will often see me here." From that moment, the pilgrimages to this sanctuary took on astonishing proportions and the miracles multiplied *ad infinitum*.

In 1665, Benoîte undertook the construction of the church. Completed in four years under the direction of the shepherdess, the new sanctuary received the name of Notre Dame du Laus. The

Our Lady appearing to Benoît Reneurel

The Infant Moses in the Basket

persecutions then began against Benoîte and against this pilgrimage. It was claimed that the new devotion to Notre Dame du Laus would destroy the ancient devotion to Notre Dame d'Embrun. The shepherdess did not despair. "The devotion of Laus," her good angel said to her, March 18, 1700, "is the work of God; neither man nor demon can destroy it; it will remain until the end of the world, it will always flower more and more, and will produce great fruits everywhere." The works continued until the death of the holy shepherdess who, at the age of seventy-one, went to receive the reward for her zeal on the day of the Holy Innocents in 1718.

Under the Reign of Terror, Notre Dame du Laus was ransacked and closed. But since then, the pilgrimage has resumed its ancient splendour.

༄༅༄

15 ~ The Basket of Moses

(Exodus 2: 1-10)

Israel groans under the yoke of the oppressor. The tyrant condemned all male children to perish in the waters of the Nile as soon as they were born. What then is this basket stopped between the reeds of the river? Fear not; the angel of the Lord watches, the waters of the river will not penetrate this fragile boat; for it is the cradle of Moses.

In vain the river of original corruption surrounded the daughter of Anne and Joachim.[39] For the honour of Him whose womb will be the cradle, *propter honorem Filii*, when it is a question of sin there can be no question of Mary. (St. Augustine).

The river of error, the river of vice surrounds the Church; but in the Church rests Jesus. He rests there by His word, by His Gospel; He rests there by His presence, by the Eucharist. Error and vice will not enter the basket of the new Moses. There will be sinners in the bosom of the Church, it is true, but the Church itself remains spotless and unblemished, holy and immaculate (Ephes 5:27);[40] just as, despite the errors of some of its members, it always remains the pillar of truth and the infallible echo of the Word of Jesus Christ.

And you, by faith in His Word and in His Vicar, and by charity, keep Jesus in your mind and in your heart: error and vice will not enter your soul.

As formerly Mary, the sister of Moses, who watched over the basket where the child lay; thus Mary will watch over your heart which has become the cradle of the Infant Jesus.

---

39   I.e. the river is symbolic of the flood of corruption caused by original sin. Out of all the children condemned to death, Moses was saved by a specially prepared vessel through which the water did not penetrate. This is symbolic of Mary. In order to be the Mother of God and give Him His most pure flesh, she had to be specially prepared, she was raised above the rest of the human race and received the grace of being immaculately conceived, untouched and unstained by corruption of any kind. There is no question that Mary was conceived without original sin.

40   "Christ also loved the church, and delivered himself up for it: (...) That he might present it to himself a glorious church, not having spot or wrinkle, or any such thing; but that it should be holy, and without blemish." (Eph. 5:25,27)

Notre Dame des Doms (Avignon)

St. Martha, together with St. Ruf, son of Simon the Cyrenean and first bishop of Avignon, raised in this city a sanctuary in honour of the Mother of God, which afterwards received the name of Notre Dame des Doms.[41] After his conversion, Constantine enlarged this pious oratory. It is said that it was near Avignon that the famous vision of the cross took place. In 731, the church of Constantine was sacked by the Saracens. Around 785, Charlemagne, called in history the great builder of churches and moutiers (of monasteries), raised this sanctuary. Jesus Christ, they say, came in person in the middle of the night to consecrate the new church. This marvellous fact was witnessed by a lady who gave proofs of what she had seen. Charlemagne had the representation of the prodigy sculpted on the capitals of the columns that supported the cloister of the church. In 1316, Pope John XXII attested to this fact in a bull. In 1475, Sixtus IV also recognized the miraculous consecration, as well as the founding of the

---

41   The church was built over an ancient pagan site called the Rocher des Doms. It is not uncommon for the first Christians to take pagan sites and claim them for God and for Christ's christian kingdom. Since the pagan gods are described as devils in the Bible, seizing pagan sites shows how victory over the world and the devil is claimed for Christ, Who overcame the world and defeated the devil, death and sin. One of the most famous examples is the Pantheon in Rome. Once dedicated to all the gods, 'pan' and 'theon', the Catholic Church claimed it for the one and only true universal God. Even St. Michael has famously appeared on pagan worship sites and claimed them for his own shrines. We have seen elsewhere in this book the early churches of France were built on the pagan temples of old.

church by St. Martha.

Among the holy personages who came to pray there, we cite St. Remi de Rheims, St. Mayeul de Cluny, St. Pons de Villeneuve, St. Hugues de Grenoble, St. Dominic, St. Peter of Luxembourg, St. Francis of Borgia, St. Francis de Sales, St. Catherine of Sienna, St. Delphine, St. Colette. This is where in 1322 John XXII ordered the daily triple ringing of the Angelus. It was near the porch of this cathedral that he received the famous apparition in which the Virgin ordered him to publish the Sabbatine bull in favour of the scapular. (The Brown scapular). Under this same porch, St. André Corsini miraculously restored sight to a blind man. At the beginning of the 15th century, for ten years, St. Vincent Ferrier did not miss a single day to sing mass there at the altar of the Virgin.

In front of the altar of Notre Dame des Doms knelt Louis VIII (1226), Charles.le-Bel (1324), the Emperor Charles IV and Duke Amédée VI of Savoy (1365), Charles VI (1388), Charles VII, still Dauphin (1420), Francis I (1516), Charles IX (1564), Henry III (1574), Catherine de Medici (1579), Marie de Medici (1600), Louis XIII, (1622), Louis XIV and his mother (1660).

In the 14th century, seven popes appeared there in all the splendour of papal majesty: Clement V, John XXII, Benedict XII, Clement VI, Innocent VI, Urban V and Gregory XI. The latter instituted the feast of the Presentation of the Blessed Virgin there.
It is in this church that the feasts of the Blessed Trinity, [42] and of the Holy Lance and of the Holy Nails were

---

42 Trinity Sunday was celebrated in the 10th century, and gradually spread to churches in northern Europe. Eventually, in 1334 Pope John XXIII established it as a universal feast day in the Church.

Notre Dames des Doms, Avignon

established;[43] it was there that the first procession of the Corpus Christi was celebrated.[44] King Philippe-le-Bel and Peter of Aragon were absolved there of the excommunication they had incurred. Finally, Pius IX took pleasure in further glorifying Notre Dame des Doms.[45]

The cult of devotion to St. Anne originated in the country of Avignon. St. Auspice, first bishop of Apt, had received from the hands of St. Lazarus the body of St. Anne. He hid it in a crypt which he made into an oratory of the Blessed Virgin. This hiding place was discovered towards the end of the 8th century and a church was built above the cave.[46] From then on, St. Anne received homage from all over Provence. Popes and kings came to pray in front of this tomb. Anne of Austria lived there with Louis XIV.

It was again in Avignon that the devotion to the spouse of Mary began. Pope Gregory XI built in the church of Saint-Agricol[47] a chapel in honour of St. Joseph, which was, it is said, the first erected to this great Saint.[48]

---

43   Innocent VI instituted the Feast of the Most Holy and Nails, which occurs the Friday after the First Sunday of Lent.
44   Pope John XIII began the first ever Corpus Christi procession in 1316.
45   Bl. Pius IX gave the cathedral the title of minor basilica in 1854.
46   Apt Cathedral, which is believed to have been built on the site where St. Auspice was buried. Tradition holds that Auspice became the custodian of the relics of Saint Anne, and placed them in a subterranean grotto to protect them from desecration by the barbarians.
47   After Notre Dame des Doms, the Collegiate Church of St Agricola is the oldest standing place of worship in Avignon. It was built in the early 1300s on the site of an older building constructed sometime between 660 and 700 by St. Agricola, venerated as the protector of crops.
48   It is also said that the first act of public devotion to St. Joseph was carried out by the Confraternity of Bachelors in

16 ~ The Burning Bush

(Exodus 3: 1-14)

What is this bush that burns without being consumed? It is Mary, surrounded by the flames of original sin which devours all else around her, but which dare not touch her; it is Mary, who became a mother without ceasing to be a virgin; it is Mary, as if enveloped in the Divinity of the Word having become her Son, and not failing to retain all her freedom.[49]

The Church is enveloped at the same time, but in a very different sense, by the world and by God.

The world surrounds it with all the flames of human passions and infernal hatreds. Like the bush, the Church remains intact within this fire.

It is that God on His side, surrounds and penetrates His Church with all the splendours, with all the lights of truth, with all the ardour, with all the flames of charity. However, these divine lights do not absorb (nullify) human lights: faith does not destroy reason. These celestial flames do not consume the legitimate inclinations of nature: charity does not abolish liberty.

The Church is divine and human. Divine, it is inaccessible to the fires of (sinful) human passion; human, it remains such, even under divine action.

Avignon, and first propagated by Gregory XI in the church of Agricola c. 1370 the time the chapel was built.

[49] i.e. she accepted to become the Mother of God of her own free will, it was not enforced upon her.

The Burning Bush

And we, we fear too much both God and the world. – We are afraid to surrender ourselves to God, as if the light and the flame of the grave were to nullify our intelligence and our natural freedom. Grace does not destroy nature, it only purifies it and elevates it. – Faith assures and increases in you the knowledge of God, of the soul and of the world: it does not take away from you anything that you can acquire by simple reason – Charity attaches you to God and delivers you from all impure affections or disorders, it frees you from the bondage of sin, it forbids you the liberty of (committing) evil, which is the most shameful slavery;

---

50   i.e. Charity, true love of God, means you wish to do His

but it assures you the freedom of good, the only true freedom. So let us surrender to God, and we will fear the world less.

This world, it is true, inspired by the devil and seconded by the flesh, (i.e. the world, the flesh and the devil), envelops us in the fires of triple lust. But if God is in you, as He was in the burning bush from which He made Himself heard to Moses, His Word and His almighty action will preserve you from all the attacks of the accursed flame.

Notre Dame de Peyragude (Diocese of Agen)

A long time ago, to the west of the Château-du-Roi, on the circular plateau from which the eye contemplates the verdant valley of Sainte-Foi-de-Penne, a young shepherdess followed the sheep of a poor small herd. Her downcast features, her distracted gaze, said enough that she was under the sway of deep pain.

---

commandments and to sin no more. While we have the free will to commit evil, we are forbidden by God's laws to commit it as a life of sin is a life of spiritual bondage, sin leads to the most base and detestable kind of slavery there is, to be a slave to corruption, and in the end, the wages of sin is eternal death and hell. "Jesus answered them: Amen, amen I say unto you: that whosoever committeth sin, is the servant of sin." (John 8:34) "Know you not, that to whom you yield yourselves servants to obey, his servants you are whom you obey, whether it be of sin unto death, or of obedience unto justice. (...) For the wages of sin is death. But the grace of God, life everlasting, in Christ Jesus our Lord." (Romans 6: 16,23) "For the law of the spirit of life, in Christ Jesus, hath delivered me from the law of sin and of death." (Romans 8:2)

Shrine at Peyragude

    The young girl let her sheep settle in these abandoned pastures, and headed for the sharp rock, which juts out from the side of the rock where the Tour-du-Roi once stood. She knelt at the foot of the rock in a narrow angle that hid her from curious eyes. Little by little hers pain broke out; her eyes filled with tears, her hands went up pleadingly, then she fell slumped. The sky was dark and cloudy; a biting wind threw light snowflakes on the child's face. Suddenly her sheep crowd around her, and a Lady, of radiant beauty, dressed in a white dress spangled with gold, bends over the shepherdess and raises her gently.

"My child," said the Lady, "fear not, and entrust your pain to me."

"Alas! Madam," the young girl responded, "our pain is hunger! I am hungry, my father and my mother are hungry."

"Well! My child, take comfort, for your prayer has risen to God. He who feeds the swallow and her young will not let the girl perish who implores Him for her parents. Get up, run, to your mother, tell her to bake a loaf for herself, a loaf for you, a loaf for your father. Then you will come and offer me a piece; I love the bread of tears."

"Madame," replied the shepherdess, "summer has fled, winter has come, the sheaf of my father's fields is exhausted; there is nothing to bake bread at home."

"My child, there will be bread in your father's house. The sheaf has given its wheat, and the dough ferments in the kneader. Run, my daughter, and bring me a piece."

The Lady spoke with such authority, her hand stretched out towards the cottage, that the shepherdess obeyed.

While listening to what she was saying, her parents thought she had gone mad. However, her assurance triumphed over their amazement. She dragged her mother away, and as the Beautiful Lady had said, the dough was overflowing, fermenting, in the poor man's old kneader.

"Yes," adds here the chronicler of these days of faith, "yes, the parable of the Lord Jesus in the Holy Gospel is true; 'Ask, and you shall receive.' This poor girl cried out to God, and God answered her. Thus we learn from the loaves multiplied in the desert, the wine of Cana, the crow of Elijah, the cake baked under the ashes, the flour of the widow of Sarephta. What is impossible for men is easy for God."

We can well imagine that there was joy in the family and a hurry to bake the miraculous bread and bring the Lady her share. They climbed light and swift up the slope of the hill. The sheep were grazing; the favourite lamb came to meet them, bleating. But the Beautiful Lady had disappeared, and had it not been for the lamb which went before them, they would not have known the source of all their happiness. At the angle of the sharp rock the little animal bent his knees and lowered his head. A celestial fragrance filled the grotto, and on the moss lay a graceful little statue of the Blessed Virgin holding the Child Jesus.

"It is the beautiful Lady! It is the Lady of Heaven! She is the one who gave us bread," cried the young shepherdess.

She removed the blessed image, carried it to the church, and made a vow at her feet to consecrate along with her innocence, her whole life to Jesus.

The next day she returned to the church to pray before the Madonna. The holy image was no longer there. Inconsolable, she flew to the rock where the day before she had had so much joy. It was there that the little statue had returned. It was understood that she wanted to have her sanctuary in this place, and it rose rapidly before the miracles and favours which Our Lady of Peyragude profusely spread. (Pierre aiguë, or sharp stone). (Excerpt from the *Guirlande de Marie*).

17 ~ The Rod of Moses

(Exodus 4: 1-4)

Moses throws his rod on the ground, it is changed into a serpent. Thus Eve, thus our soul, thus the whole human family, by affection for earthly and tangible things, becomes devious, creeping and poisonous like the serpent.

Moses then picks up his rod. It becomes straight and firm again. Thus Mary, thus the faithful and just soul, so the Church, is upright and firm under the hand of God, by faith which straightens and strengthens the reason, by virtue which straightens and strengthens the will.

Ten times Moses lifts his rod, and ten times the scourge of the liberating God falls upon the oppressor. (The ten plagues of Egypt.)

Pray to Mary, pray ten times, pray always, (for) your soul: the passion that enslaves you, and also the Pharaoh oppressing the Church, the Caesar that oppresses the Christian people, will then be scourged. Because Mary by the very fact that she is a Mother, is also a powerful and terrible queen like an army arrayed in battle to defend her children.

Moses raises his rod and a great wind opens a passage to Israel through the waves. (Exodus 14:16) Moses lifts his rod and the waves come together to swallow up Pharaoh's warriors, steeds and chariots.

Moses striking the rock

The head of the Church invokes Mary, (the pope), and a breath from above opens for the new people of God a passage through the waves of the passions of the flesh and the world; also through the bloody flood of revolution, and closing over the heads of the (modern day) Pharaohs, engulfs them in the abyss.

The rod of Moses touches the rock and from this arid rock springs a spring of living water. (Exodus 17:5-6)

Your heart, were it as hard as dry as rock, or, the heart of a sinner whom you wish to convert, were it as insensitive as stone, invoke Mary, and from this heart will spring the tears of repentance.

But this stone also represents Jesus Himself. *Petra autem erat Christus.* ("And the rock was Christ", 1 Cor. 10:4)

Invoke Mary, she has the sovereign power of a mother over the heart of her Son, she will open this Divine Heart and there will spring from it a font of living water, an abundance of grace which will spread throughout the whole Church and which will revive in each of its members the spiritual life, the supernatural life, principle and pledge of eternal life: *Fons aquae salientis in vita aeternam.* ("But the water that I will give him, shall become in him a fountain of water, springing up into life everlasting." John 4:14)

Notre Dame du Puy[51]

It was under the pontificate of St. Vosy, (bishop of Puy) in the 3rd century:

> "A Christian woman was afflicted with an incurable disease which left her no rest, nothing could ease her sufferings except praying to Mary whom she loved with all her soul. One night she heard a voice telling her to go to the peak of Anis and there to await her orders; she had herself carried to the designated place on the mountain.[52]

---

51 Also called Puy-d'Anis or Puy-en-Velay.
52   Here we have another instance of Heaven claiming back a pagan site. Our Lady instructed the sick women to lay down on a dolmen stone where a pagan temple once stood. It has since been called the 'fever stone' and is still visible in a

"Soon, a sweet sleep seizes her senses; during this mysterious slumber, the Virgin appeared to her in the midst of a troop of Angels and said to her: 'My daughter, you are healed and your prayers have been heard; go to Vosy, my servant and your bishop, and tell him on my behalf that he build on this mountain the sanctuary of Puy-d'Anis; this is the place that I have chosen among a thousand to listen favourably to those who will want to bring me their prayers and their requests.'

"The celestial vision disappeared; the patient hastened to fulfil the mission which she had received and which God still wished to confirm by a new miracle; in the month of July the mountain is covered with snow, and a deer marks out the plan of a church with its prints. St. Vosy hastens, he sees the miracle and builds the sanctuary of which, by an inspiration from Heaven, he predicts its future glory. The piety of the faithful, the visits of saints, great personages and peoples have taken care of verifying this oracle.

"It is under the current copula where the "angelic chamber" is, made famous by so many miraculous occurrences."

---

little chapel next to the Marian choir. St. Vosy and St. Scutaire erected the sanctuary housing the dolmen on the ruins of a former pagan temple. It believed the 'Salve Regina' was first composed here in Puy-en-Velay as it has been attributed to Adhémar, Bishop of Podium (Puy-en-Velay), whence it has been styled "Antiphona de Podio" (Anthem of Le Puy).

The 'fever stone' at Notre Dame du Puy

"St. Vosy had been helped with the construction of the building by St. Scrutaire, well versed in the art of architecture and who was himself to become bishop of Velay. The building finished, they wanted to consecrate and dedicate it; for this they have recourse to the Apostolic See which is the centre of unity and they leave for Rome. Scarcely had the two travellers journeyed half an hour, (and the precise place of this halt, several stones still designate it), than they saw coming towards them two venerable old men whose clothes were white as snow and who carried two precious vases. 'Go no further,' say the elders, 'God has already provided for the dedication of your sanctuary; take these relics and retrace your steps, your church is now consecrated by the Angels.' Our two Saints ascend the blessed mountain in all haste; O prodigy! The bells ring, the tunes resound with harmonious hymns, thousands of candles burn around the sanctuary, the altar is still moistened with the holy oil which an invisible power had poured upon it, and the temple is filled with the odour of celestial perfumes.

"Our Lady of Puy d'Anis therefore became a place of pilgrimage visited by the Sovereign Pontiffs, among others Urban II, and where emperors and kings flocked; Charlemagne visited these blessed places three times, St. Louis IX went there before and after the crusade; it is he who brought to the sanctuary the miraculous statue of the Black Virgin. Alas! Sad memory of 1793! (The Revolution.) Sacrilegious hands burned it. The image that we have today is however a very faithful representation and produces the same wonders; Mary forgave the crime.[53]

"Louis XI made the pilgrimage to Notre Dame du Puy d'Anis three times, the third time so as not to die; arriving at Fix, he wanted to come on foot, walked for twenty kilometres and wore for three hours the surplice and the *aumusse* of the canons.

---

[53] The Black Virgin is venerated especially on the 25th. March, the day of the Annunciation, and on the 15th. August, feast of the Assumption. The statue is carried in procession by local inhabitants through the streets of Le Puy.

The Black Virgin of Puy

– Charles VII, when abandoned by everyone, even by his mother, came here to seek refuge. He was proclaimed king on the rock of Espaly, close to Mont d'Anis.

"One wonders why the double term of Notre Dame du Puy and Notre Dame de France! Notre Dame de France is the affirmation of the devotion that France wants to render to Mary, it is in one of its great manifestations of national devotion. Notre Dame du Puy is the local devotion; for a long time, for more than twelve centuries, our Virgin has been venerated under the name of Notre Dame de France; pilgrims flocked there from everywhere, even from the very depths of Africa. Le Puy, by Mary, is the heart of France.

"In the past, on the Rock of Corneille, there was a weather vane, today religion has placed there the colossal statue of Notre Dame de France and for the mind attentive to the grandeur and the conduct of the project, this was not done without a badge of protection from Heaven.... The proposed statue was to represent three symbols; the Immaculate Conception, the Divine Motherhood, the Royalty of Mary. A skilful workman was needed, an artist presented himself, M. Bonnassieux. Money was needed, Mgr de Morlhon had confidence in France and alms were plentiful; the national devotion had to be consecrated, he went to Napoleon III, and obtained his subscription and that of the Empress; he asked him about the material for the statue, the cannons of Sevastopol which were not yet taken .... The Emperor is surprised, smiles and promises;[54] two days later, our victorious armies ensured the fulfilment of this promise."

(*Extract from the 'Récit des Gloires de Notre Dame du Puy', by M. de Pélacot, Vicar General of the Congrès de l'Union des Oeuvres in 1877*).

ಐ ❀ ಐ

18 ~ The Pillar of Cloud

(Exodus 14: 19-20)

Cloud during the day, fire during the night, the mysterious column which accompanies Israel, defends it by day against the heat of the sun, by night against the surprises of the enemy; obscure on the side of the Egyptians, it does not allow them to advance against the people of God; luminous on the side of the Hebrews, it reassures them against night terrors.

---

54 I.e. he asked for the metal from the cannons of Sevastopol after the victory of the army when they take the town, therefore, in faith he asked before they had even secured the town. The army proved victorious and the metal was given.

*Joshua passing the River Jordan
with the Ark of the Covenant*

Mary is both a gentle and tender mother for her children, a powerful and formidable queen against their adversaries. She defends her children against the ardour of passion and against the surprises of the enemy whom she arrests and blinds at the same time.

The sages and powerful of Egypt, (and now), the princes of this age, the so-called philosophers and the so-called politicians want to confine the children of God to what they call modern ideas and principles; they thought they already had them in the maze and the network of their laws as petty as they are perverse. But the Church, luminous for docile minds and for pure hearts, arrests the sages and the prudent of this world by the obscurities of faith.[55] They were worthy to lose the light and to be locked up in darkness, those who kept locked up the children of God. ("Therefore they received a burning pillar of fire for a guide of the way which they knew not, and thou gavest them a harmless sun of a good entertainment. The others indeed were worthy to be deprived of light, and imprisoned in darkness, who kept thy children shut up, by whom the pure light of the law was to be given to the world." Wisdom 18:3-4)

Notre Dame de Grâce (Cambrai)

Cambrai is given the name of Ville de la Virgin. It is a suitable name for it.

The ancient Gallic city, Cameracum, received the faith in the first century, even envoys of St. Peter, companions of Saint Denis; and from the day when the young Christian city bent the knee before the cross, Mary, mother of the Crucified, stretched her powerful hand over it.

After the barbarian invasions, the Cambresian metropolis rose from its ruins through the care of its bishop St. Waast, disciple of St. Remy and catechist of Clovis.

---

55   i.e. what is bright and clear for the true children of God through faith appears dark and obscure to the worldly-wise who do not have faith. They lose the light of faith and will suffer darkness similar to the Egyptians of old.

Cambrai revived at the same time in the same waters where the proud Sicambre found life. (496 AD).[56]

We will not here follow every detail of the rapid growth of the devotion of Mary in these regions. Note however that from the eleventh century her name is honoured in all of northern France; it is that of Notre Dame de Cambrai, Notre Dame la Grande.

The lords of Cambrésis paid homage to her as to their queen. The people hailed her as their safeguard. St. Bernard, inspired by the spirit of God who spread miracles and benefits through her hands, came to pray to her and said mass at her altar. St. Louis IX learned to invoke her, and as a mark of his trust and respect, he sent her a golden crown enriched with precious stones. Rosebeck's flags were placed at her feet.[57]

---

56   I.e. this is possibly a reference to the conversion of baptism of King Clovis, who was referred to by St. Remy as a Sicamber, a member of the Sicambri, also known as the Sugambri or Sicambrians, a Germanic people who during Roman times lived on the east bank of the river Rhine. By the 3rd century, the region in which they and their neighbours had lived had become part of the territory of the Franks, which was a new name that possibly represented a new alliance of older tribes. The term Frank (for French Franks) later than became synonymous with being called Sicambers, and *vice versa*.

57   No doubt a reference to the Battle of Rosebeck during the Ghent Rebelion (1379- 1385), and the One Hundred Years War (1337-1453). It is also spelled Roosebeke, and sometimes referred by its contemporary name as Battle of Westrozebeke. The French won the battle and apparently, the flags of the enemy were laid in thanksgiving at the feet of Our Lady of Cambrai.

Public devotion to her is a political one.[58] Coins are struck with her effigy, her image, a sacred palladium, represents her standing, crowned, holding the sceptre in her hand; her left arm surrounds the child Jesus seated on the escutcheon with three lions of the county of Cambrésis. The Sovereign relies on the arms of her kingdom.

Thus did faith penetrate all things. Jesus Christ reigned.

In the year of Our Lord, 1440, a canon from the metropolis of Cambrai, Fursy de Bruille, was in Rome.

He was about to leave the pontifical city when one of the princes of the Holy Church presented himself to him, saying that, in obedience to a revelation from God, he wanted to donate to the Metropolitan Church of Cambrai a precious treasure of which he was the custodian.

This treasure was the image of Our Lady of Grace that we venerate today.

Theodore, lector of the church of Constantinople about the year 530 AD, relates that in the times which followed the conversion of Constantine, there was sent to the empress of Constantine and to the empress Pulchérie, granddaughter of the great Theodosius, a portrait of the Most Holy Virgin Mary, preserved until that time in Jerusalem, where the Mother of

---

58 i.e. it is shown publicly in the secular administration of the region.

Notre Dame de Grâce

God lived, and which the Christian tradition of that city attributed to the brush of the Evangelist St. Luke.

Pulcheria built a temple where she placed the Holy Image, which immediately became the object of great veneration for the faithful of the imperial city.

Towards the middle of the 15th century when the Mohammedan armies invaded the Eastern Roman Empire, people hastened to remove and transport relics and precious objects to the West. Among them was the image of Our Lady of Grace. Brought to Rome, delivered into faithful hands, Divine Providence destined it as a pledge of its divine protection for the lands of northern France so full of faith and piety.

The Cambraisiens were faithful to their mission, they preciously deposited the holy image in the old cathedral of Cambrai, a masterpiece of Gothic art, which was called "the wonder of the North" and which the minions of Joseph Lebon destroyed in the disastrous days of the First Republic.

We were then, as we have said, in the middle of the fifteenth century, in the year 1450. Flanders, Hainaut, Picardy, Ostrevant immediately rushed to contemplate these features copied from the holy original itself.

From 1454, Bruges sent the first of the painters of its famous school to make three copies, and the devotion to Our Lady of Grace spread in the Belgian provinces.

In 1557, Philippe le Bon, Duke of Burgundy, begged for her protection and offered her gifts.

Louis XI hung from the vault of her sanctuary a large crown adorned with twelve silver candlesticks, on which was placed the following inscription: "The year of the Incarnation one thousand four hundred LXXVIII Louis XI of the name, king of France on which all honour shines, founded here the aforesaid year to decorate the Mother of Grace: let us pray day and night to Jesus that no soul should perish."

In 1529, the 'Paix des Dames' was signed in Cambrai. It was at the foot of the miraculous Image that the treaty was ratified.

And so, it all comes down to this blessed sanctuary. Cambrai and Notre Dame de Grâce, it is the same love, the same patriotism, the same devotion. Her image dominates the main door of the town hall. Four of the gates of the city are placed under her protection. In the streets, on the houses her features appear, reproduced in sculpture and painting.

And when, in the years 1649 and 1657, on two different occasions, defenceless Cambrai was besieged by victorious enemies, and when, after having spent the night at the feet of their Patroness, our fore fathers suddenly saw themselves twice miraculously delivered, enthusiasm was then at its height.

By Our Lady of Grace, Cambrai is delivered, so say the commemorative medallions struck at that time, the profusion of which that the momentum of recognition alone can explain: "Condeo Urbem libranti; by Our Lady of Grace, his Highness Condé Cambrai delivered;" Condé, who, on entering the city of which he had just raised the siege, did not wish to dismount except at the very threshold of the sanctuary of Our Lady of Grace.[59]

And the surrounding regions rushed to thank She, who by saving Cambrai, also saved them.

Three thousand Valenciennes offer a golden lamp on which were seen the patrons of the three parishes of the city, St. Vaast, St. Nicolas, St. Jacques. An inscription recalls the occasion of this gift. "In vain," it said, "the enemy attacks a city of which Mary is the Protector.... The inhabitants donated this lamp to Notre Dame de Grâce, because by delivering Cambrai, she also saved Valenciennes from enemy fury." Seven thousand pilgrims came from Douay. Bouchain brought a monumental candle with this motto: "To Our Lady of Grace, for the deliverance of Cambrai, the year 1657, the people of

---

[59] In June of 1657, the Prince of Condé lifted the siege of Cambrai during the Anglo-Spanish war of 1654-1660.

Bouchain."

From 1649 to 1660, festivals and pilgrimages followed one after the another. It was a long cry of gratitude to She whose all powerful hand had stopped the victorious armies.

As liberated Israel sang the glory of Judith, so the city of the Virgin celebrated the praises of the modern Judith in whom, in hours of danger, it had placed its trust and hope.

The image of Our Lady of Grace was placed in the Chapel of the Holy Trinity, above the altar. We still have the stone of this altar on which Fénelon[60] celebrated the Holy Mass every day."

(Extract from Pèlerin.)

---

[60] François de Salignac de la Mothe-Fénelon (1651-1715), more commonly known as François Fénelon, was a French Catholic archbishop, theologian, poet and writer. He is remembered mostly as the author of 'The Adventures of Telemachus' published in 1699.

19 ~ The Rock of Horeb

(Exodus 17:6)

Where shall we flee? Into the desert? But we cannot live there. Water is lacking. Yet, go always: for there you will encounter the stone of Horeb.

From the top of His cross, Jesus, the new Moses, touched the heart of Mary. "Woman," He said to her, while glancing at the beloved disciple, "there is your son." And suddenly from the Heart of Mary, from this Heart that at the foot of the cross showed itself firmer than rock, from this Heart springs an inexhaustible font of maternal tenderness that will be for all men a font of grace and eternal life.

So also the Church, built on rock, pours the waters of grace over the world through the sacraments.

Revived by these marvellous waters, you will cross the desert of life, you will arrive at Sinai.

Notre Dame d'Avesnières

"Avesnières, one kilometre from Laval, is strictly speaking a suburb of this city. The church of this borough, dedicated to the Virgin, is one of the most beautiful monuments of the region. For centuries many pilgrims have visited this revered

Notre Dame d'Avesnières

sanctuary, founded around the middle of the 11th century by Guy II, Lord of Laval, to fulfil a vow.

"As he was riding on the Mayenne bridge, his horse stumbled, throwing them together into the river. The Baron, carried away by the current and seeing that he was about to perish, commended himself to Mary. He promised to dedicate a chapel to God in her honour, at the very place where she would bring him home safe and sound. His prayer was answered. He was able to find land about a thousand paces from the place where he had begun this perilous navigation in a field of oats, where a statue of the Virgin first struck his gaze that was placed in the hollow of an oak tree by the pious inhabitants. Faithful to his vow, he built a chapel on this bank where the statue was transported, and it is believed that this church and this statue are those that exist today.

"The church of Notre Dame d'Avesnières shared in the misfortune of the country in the disastrous days of the English invasion. In one of their incursions during the 13th century, they set fire to it and burned the entire front part of the nave, which, according to an interesting report by. E.A. Segretain, would then have been diminished during its construction in the following century, and would not be rebuilt on the same plan. The church of Avesnières had been erected into a priory, and the Benedictines of Ronceray d'Angers were established there; they had the church repaired and enlarged with the proceeds of the plenary indulgences that Pope Innocent III granted in 1207 to those who came to pray there on Fridays.

"Abandoned during the Revolution, this church was the first in the vicinity of Laval to be returned to worship in 1800, and it contains the remains of fourteen priests whom the Revolution had delivered to the executioner in the public square of Laval. Since 1841, it counts among its historical monuments; the choir of the building is from the period of the transition from Romanesque to Gothic, the front part is a work of the 15th century, finally the tower and the spire were erected in 1534."

(Extract from the *Le Dimanche Illustré* de Toulouse.)

20 ~ Mount Sinai

(Exodus 19)

Do not touch the mountain. Death would be the punishment for your temerity.[61] – Likewise, do not insult Mary, it would be the death of your soul.

A thick cloud covered Sinai and in this cloud thunders resound and the lightning flashes are dominated by the formidable brilliance of the great voice of God. – Thus on the day of the Incarnation the virtue of the Most High shrouded Mary in its shadow. *Virtus Altissimi obumbrabit tibi.* ("And the power of the Most High shall overshadow thee." Luke 1:35)

But if Mt. Sinai appears dark, dreadful, shrouded in smoke, furrowed with lightning and thundering, it is for the proud ones who would like to climb and see beyond the limits set by God Himself: *transcendere termino ad videndum Dominum,* ("Go down, and charge the people: lest they should have a mind to pass the limits to see the Lord," Exod. 19:21); it is for carnal souls; *bestia tetigerit montem* ("And if so much as a beast shall touch the mount, it shall be stoned." Heb,

---

[61] "The Lord said to him: Lo, now will I come to thee in the darkness of a cloud, that the people may hear me speaking to thee, and may believe thee for ever. And Moses told the words of the people to the Lord. And he said to him: Go to the people, and sanctify them today, and tomorrow, and let them wash their garments. And let them be ready against the third day: for on the third day the Lord will come down in the sight of all the people upon mount Sinai. And thou shalt appoint certain limits to the people round about, and thou shalt say to them: Take heed you go not up into the mount, and that ye touch not the borders thereof: every one that toucheth the mount dying he shall die." (Exod. 19: 9-12)

12:18); but to men of faith, to pure hearts, Mt. Sinai is like a serene sky: *quasi coelum cum serenum est.* ("and as the heaven, when clear," Exod. 24:10)[62]

This is an image of Mary, who shows herself formidable to proud minds and sensual hearts, but gentle and serene to the humble and the innocent.

This is an image of the Church: the haughty minds who pretend to see everything and explain everything by reason, find only darkness and smoke in the high and pure teachings of the Church; carnal hearts understand absolutely nothing about it. For some as for others, the Church has only flashes and thunderbolts. But for those minds which faith elevates, for those hearts which charity purifies, the doctrine of the Church is a pure heaven, calm and serene.

God descends on Mt. Sinai: He descends in Mary by the Incarnation; He descends into the Church by the Eucharist; He descends into the faithful soul through Holy Communion.

From the top of Sinai, God gives His law to Israel. – Mary, whose name signifies elevation, is the mountain from the top of which God gives to the whole world He Who is the Living Law, the Word which, made incarnate in the womb of the Immaculate Virgin, will be revealed by the Gospels and by the Church.

Three times God made a covenant with man: first in the earthly paradise with Adam, father and head of the human family; then on Sinai with Moses, saviour and leader of a chosen people, finally, in the womb of Mary by the union of the Divine nature and human nature in the person of Jesus Christ.

---

[62] "Then Moses and Aaron, Nadab and Abiu, and seventy of the ancients of Israel went up: And they saw the God of Israel: and under His feet as it were a work of sapphire stone, and as the heaven, when clear." (Exodus 24: 9-10)

Moses on Mount Sinai

This last covenant continues and is consummated in the Church.

At the summit of Sinai, Moses spoke and God answered him. At the summit of the Church, Peter speaks and God assures him of infallibility, (the pope). Let us remain united to Peter and we too will be infallible, that is infallible by faith, with the very infallibility that was guaranteed to Peter by Jesus, infallible with the infallibility of the Word Who is God.

Mary in Anjou

"We approach this diocese with a double happiness," writes M. Hamon, "firstly because there is none about which we have been better informed; secondly, because there are few others, if any, where the Blessed Virgin has been so loved, where this love has resulted in so many sacrifices and where, to expand devotion to her and to perpetuate it from age to age, so many churches, abbeys, priories, chapels.

The Angevins call the Blessed Virgin Notre Dame l'Angevine: first, because, seeing in her a mother, they like to imagine her as forming with them only one family and one people; second, because touched by her tenderness and her benefits, they regard her as belonging more especially to them than to any other people: she is eminently Angevine, and l'Angevine is her name."

(*Notre Dame de France*, vol. IV, p. 187)

L'Angevine

The feast of the nativity of Mary in that region is called 'Angevine' because according to a revelation received by St. Maurille, bishop of Angers, it was in Angers around the year 430 AD that the birth of the

Blessed Virgin was celebrated for the first time in the Church.[63]

However, on the 8th of September 732 AD, the Angevin festival acquired a new celebrity. That same day, Charles Martel won his great victory over Abdérame, which earned him his glorious nickname, and on the very evening of the battle, he instituted the order of the Knights of Genêt in honour of Mary. He only admitted with him twenty-nine warriors chosen from among those who had distinguished themselves the most on that famous day. The knights of this new order wore a gold collar of three interlaced chains with the emblem of the rose of Jericho supporting the humble flower of the shrub, with the motto: *Et*

---

[63] According to a pious tradition handed down in Angers, St. Maurille, (St. Maurilius) (c. 336 – 453) was the first to have instituted public devotion to Our Lady's nativity on September 8th. Some accounts say this is due to a revelation given to a man c. 430 AD. On the night of the 8th, the man heard the angels singing in heaven, and asking the reason, they replied they were rejoicing because the Virgin was born on that night. A text from 1638 also relates this tradition in that St. Maurilius was the first to declare in France the feast of the nativity of Our Lady be celebrated on September 8th according to a revelation, but the text states he had received it, yet without giving the details of the nature of revelation. (Source: *"Historical calendar of the Glorious Virgin Mary, mother of God"*, by Pierre Doriou, (1638). However, tradition also states it was Our Lady herself who came to him in a vision bearing the Christ child and asked him to celebrate September the 8th. The exact spot where this happened is at the Sanctuaire Notre Dame du Marillais which was built to commemorate the vision. (See Chapter 28 – Notre Dame de Marillais). Some scholars dispute this as there is no proof this happened and they conclude it is only a pious legend, especially as it seems this devotion was more widespread in the eastern church and spread from there. The visions of Bl. Catherine Emmerick states the date of September 8th as the true date of her nativity was also mystically revealed to the monks on Mt. Carmel.

exaltavit humiles; 'He exalted the humble'.[64]

On the 8th of September 1022, King Robert raised this order as Our Lady of the Star, because he substituted a star for the flower of the broom shrub, saying that Mary was the star of France. Some other modifications were made to the costume of the knights, and they were required to recite fifty Ave Marias every

---

64   Fr de Boylesve, or the source he used, may have mixed up two chivalric orders bearing similar names. The 'Order of the Genet' allegedly founded by Charles Martel has no historical basis in fact. Sources that say this order was a fabricated piece of history that first appeared centuries later in 1620 when Andre Favyn stated without giving a source the 'details' of this order in his text *'Le Théâtre d'honneur et de chevalerie, ou l'Histoire des ordres militaires des roys et princes... de l'institution des armes et blasons... duels, joustes et tournois et de tout ce qui concerne le faict du chevalier de l'ordre.'* (Robert Fouet, Paris). This text states Charles Martel had discovered a considerable number of live genets as well as a large amount of their pelts in the loot of the Muslim army he had defeated, so he made a present of the furs to his nobles and formed the first order of knights in France called the Order of the Genet. Proof of this being a fake order is that the story was consistently used to support the theory of how genets were introduced in Europe through the Arab invasions, but there was no trace of the species of genet associated with the Arabs in France at that time, and the only known archaeological remains of genets in Europe dates back to the Almohad Arab dynasty in Portugal in the thirteenth century, not France, and certainly long after the time of Charles Martel. (Source: 'Fate of the Mongooses and the Genet (Carnivora) in Mediterranean Europe: None Native, All Invasive?' by Francesco M. Angelici, published in the journal *Problematic Wildlife*. 2015 Sep 21 : 295–314.) From what I can find, historians note the details of this fabricated order were then embellished upon by other writers and scholars as time went on.

On the other hand, there was an order called the 'Colle de Genet' or 'Collar of the Broom', also known as the 'Order of

day.⁶⁵

Finally in 1243, Innocent IV made the feast of the Nativity obligatory, in accordance with the wish of the conclave where he was elected, to obtain the triumph of the Church over the factions which threatened to obstruct the election.⁶⁶

However the bishops of Angers, the counts of Anjou and the kings of France did not cease to multiply

---

the Broom-cod', i.e. as in the genet broom bush, which was founded by St. Louis IX in 1234 on the occasion of his marriage. (Although other sources claim it was founded by King Charles the Beloved.) It was not an order of chivalry, but rather, a new order of honorary distinction. A gold collar bearing broom flowers intertwined with fleur-de-lys was worn, these flowers as well as a hand holding a crown with the motto *"Extaltat homilies"* - he exalts the humble - were embroidered on the coats of the one hundred nobles who were his bodyguards who were made members of this order. The broom flower represents humility and neatness. The order was held in high esteem and being allowed to wear the broom flower was regarded as a high honour.

65   Fr. de Boylesve was again inaccurate here, or his source: the Order of the Star, *Ordre de l'Étoile,* was indeed a true order, but was a completely new order founded by King John II in 1351 in imitation of King James of England founding the Order of the Garter, although it was also called the 'Order of Our Lady of the Noble House'. Still, the star represented that which the Three Kings followed to Bethlehem, and not as a direct reference to Our Lady. The Order of the Star was not popularly received in the beginning, and, some of its rules regarding 'heroic' war tactics declaring a knight could only retreat a certain distance from the scene of a battle cost the lives of many of its knights, and led to the imprisonment of King John II himself. The order fell into further unpopularity due to this, but then, the nominal orders grew until the time of Charles V (1338-1380) to the point it made receiving the order meaningless, another disastrous effect. In all, the order was a short-lived one, and obviously, not much of a success. Fr. de Boylesve must have read a text

in this country the signs of their devotion towards Mary.

Out of twenty-two towns that comprised the old Anjou, nineteen honoured Mary as their patroness and even as their founder, since it was her chapel which, by attracting the crowd, had given birth to the first dwellings. Of nineteen abbeys, eleven had been founded in honour of Mary.

In Angers itself, out of thirty-one churches, sixteen were dedicated to the Blessed Virgin. From the top of the cathedral, placed at the centre on an eminence, Mary looks over the whole city: *totam prospicit urbem.* Since 1612 her statue was above the three main gates, with various inscriptions. On the gate of the old charter one read: *Protegam civitatem hanc propter nomen meum et propter te.* (IV. Reg. XIV, 34.) On the gate of the Montée Saint-Maurice one read: *Tu gloria Jerusalem, tu honorificentia populi nostri.* (Judith, 14:10). Finally, on the Angevin door read: *Dominare nostri tu et filius tuus.* (Judith 8:22)

෨෯෬

---

that tried to amend the unfortunate history of the Order of the Star by tying it either to the mythical Order of the Genet attributed to Charles Martel, the so-called 'first' order of chivalry in France, or, to St. Louis' honorary order to make it appear it had some glory attributed to it at least.

66   It remained a day of obligation until 1918.

21 ~ The Ark of the Covenant

(Exodus 25: 10, 16)

God gave the people of Israel a permanent sign of His covenant. This sign was an ark constructed of incorruptible wood, and covered inside and out with plates of very pure gold. (Exod. 25:10).

Here you can recognize Mary, immaculate in her conception, inviolable in her virginity. Mary is clothed with double charity: within by the love of God, of Jesus who rests in her bosom; outside, by the love of men who have become her adopted children.

Like the ark and like Mary, the Church is incorruptible: infallible in truth, immaculate in holiness: *Non habens maculam neque rugam.* ("That he might present it to himself a glorious church, not having spot or wrinkle, or any such thing; but that it should be holy, and without blemish." Ephe. 5:27) It is as if invested with the gold of double charity, of zeal for the glory of God and for the salvation of souls.

Faithful soul, be you also incorruptible and pure in your faith and in your life; put on double charity, act only for the glory of God and for the salvation of your neighbour.

The Cathedral of Angers

According to a respectable tradition, Defensor, prince or governor of Le Mans, having been converted by St. Julien,[67] became the first bishop of Angers. He dedicated his first church to the Blessed Virgin, which was later replaced by a larger and more elegant building. This new cathedral was consecrated by St. Martin of Tours under the patronage of Mary. The saint, having donated to this church a reliquary which contained the blood of St. Maurice, the people designated the cathedral by the name of this glorious chief of the Thebean legion, and this title prevailed.[68]

Overturned several times, the cathedral of Angers was rebuilt with the help of Pépin (750 AD), Charlemagne, Louis le Débonnaire and Charles le Chauve. Mary received the tributes of Kings Philippe-

---

67 St. Julian of Le Mans was believed to be a nobleman and was consecrated a bishop at Rome and around the middle of the 3rd century, Julian was sent to Gaul to bring Christianity to Cenomani tribe. Their capital city was *Civitas Cenomanorum* (Le Mans), which was suffering from a shortage of drinking water. St. Julian thrust his staff into the ground and prayed, water gushed out of the ground. This miracle allowed him to preach freely within Le Mans. Defensor converted to Christianity along with his family, donating to the Church part of his palace to serve as Le Mans' first cathedral church.

68 Although Angers Cathedral was originally dedicated to Our Lady, some sources say it was St. Martin of Tours who gave it the second dedication to St. Maurice in 396 AD, one of the commanders of the the Theban legion and martyred with them for refusing to sacrifice to the emperor.

Auguste, St. Louis IX, Charles VII, Louis XI, Charles VIII, Louis XII, Francis I, Henri II, Charles IX, Henri III, Henri IV, Louis XIII and Louis XIV. This last, by a judgment of 1670, declares that this church is called the chapel of the kings.

Notre Dame du Ronceray

After the Angers Cathedral, the region had nine other monuments of its devotion to the Blessed Virgin.

The first was the Abbey of Notre Dame of Ronceray, so named for three reasons:[69]

---

[69] **Note**: Fr. de Boylesve has extracted this information almost as is from a book by André Jean Marie Hamon entitled 'Notre-Dame de France ou Histoire du culte de la Sainte Vierge en France, depuis l'origine du christianisme jusqu'à nos jours' (1864).

Hamon does not list these events or these three reasons in chronological order. The founding charter of the abbatia Beata Maria Caritatis ("Abbey of Our Lady of Charity") at Ronceray dates from 1028. The foundation of this Benedictine abbey is attributed to Hildegarde, second wife of Foulques III, Count of Anjou. The construction is said to have been completed in 1119 when Pope Calixte II came to consecrate the main altar. Unfortunately, I cannot find a source recounting Hildegarde finding the statue at the time of the abbey's construction, but, there is a miracle attributed to a bronze statue of the Virgin found years later, (see the next footnote). An ancient text states Hildegarde eventually entered the abbey and became a nun. During the eleventh century it was the only female religious house in the area, while some sources say it only accepted women from the nobility, others says women of lower status were also admitted among the sisters. It became a famous centre for learning and members of the nobility sent their daughters there for their education. It was one of the most influential convents in France in the Middle Ages.

1st, a bramble came out of the wall, pierced the lozenges of the panes, and went to embrace and caress the statue of Mary on her altar: it was cut, they tried to pull it out, it always grew back.[70]

2Nd, in the early days of evangelical preaching, the Christians of Angers gathered in this place in an underground chapel. The pagans, having learned of this, came to massacre them there; but in the place of the chapel they saw only brambles and thorns, and they could not discover the faithful.[71]

3rd, Countess Hildegarde, believing herself suspected of infidelity by her husband Foulques Nerra, threw herself into the Maine in order to prove her innocence.[72] She had promised God that if she escaped

---

70 Apparently, this happened in the abbey crypt in 1527: the ancient crypt from the 6th century had been walled up and lost until then, and when it was opened, they discovered a bronze statue of the Blessed Virgin covered in brambles, but the foot of the statue always remained green. Perhaps, this gave rise to the legend the brambles 'kissed' the statue as it remained unharmed all that time and only the foot seemed 'touched' in a humble manner. The name 'Ronceray' was not given to it until this discovery occurred.

71 Unfortunately, I cannot find any other information regarding the first Christian settlement that was saved from the pagans by the bramble bushes except from Hamon's book, which Fr. de Boylesve used as his source. Hamon does not give his source.

72 I have not been able to find any information as to this miraculous escape other than Hamon's book, but, it has been recounted in historical sources her husband was infamous for his cruelty, he undertook several pilgrimages to the Holy Land, and, apparently, built many religious sites in reparation for his deeds. For instance, one of his dastardly acts included having his first wife unjustly tried and burnt at the stake as she failed to give him an heir. If there is any truth to the pious legend of the abbey's founding as told by Fr. de Boylesve, perhaps Hildegarde feared the same fate would happen to her.

Altar of the Virgin in the crypt chapel
Trinity Church - Ronceray

death she would raise a sanctuary to the Virgin with a monastery of religious wherever she landed. God took pity on her simplicity. She landed at the place where Le Ronceray is today. But then the old chapel of the first Christians had disappeared. Together with the Count of Anjou, even more convinced of her innocence than, moreover, he had never suspected, Hildegarde sets out to fulfil this vow. While digging the foundations, the workers found in a bramble bush a copper statuette which represented the Blessed Virgin seated on a throne and holding the Infant Jesus on her knees. "Oh!" said the Countess, "here is Notre Dame of Ronceray." They dug again and discovered a well-vaulted underground chapel, supported by two rows of pillars, twelve on each side. Above this sanctuary was erected the church that the countess had made a vow to construct.[73]

---

[73] From the information I can find, the abbey was built on the site of an ancient Merovingian sanctuary dating from the 6th-century that was constructed on an ancient crypt. A Mass was celebrated there in c. 529 AD by St. Melaine, Archbishop of Rennes, who was assisted by St. Aubin, bishop of Angers, St. Victor, Bishop of Le Mans, St. Laud, bishop of Coutances, and St. Mars, bishop of Nantes. ('*L'Église Abbatiale du Ronceray d'Angers: Ètude Archéologique*', by Lefèvre-Pontalis, (Henri Delesques, Caen, 1912. p. 4) There is an interesting pious legend that St. Melaine had invited all the bishops to the region, which is why they where all together in the ancient chapel that would day be part of the Abbey of Ronceray and assisted at St. Melaine's Mass. Each had prepared a special eulogy, and St. Melaine had given each blessed bread in brotherly charity. According to one account it was customary to give blessed bread and say eulogies after Mass on such grand occasions. St. Mars, however, realized it was Ash Wednesday, and therefore a day of fast. He refused to eat the bread, and hid it under his cloak. Heaven apparently was not pleased with this as it was a rejection of fraternal charity given to him in hospitality, for the bread

The statue of Notre Dame of Ronceray was hidden during the Revolution of 1793. Today it is in the church of the Trinity on the altar of the Virgin.

ಸಾ ✿ ಯ

22 ~ The Law, the Manna, the Rod

(Hebr. 9:4)

The Ark contained three things: the tablets of the Law written by the hand of God, a vessel of gold filled with the miraculous manna of the desert, the rod of the high priest that had flowered by a prodigy.

In the womb of Mary I adore the Living Law, Wisdom and Justice Itself, the Legislator in person; I adore the One who will call Himself and make Himself the true manna, the Living Bread descended from

---

turned into a serpent, while other accounts say it was his eulogy that turned into the serpent. Recognizing his sin, he begged St. Malaine for forgiveness, and the serpent transformed back into the bread, or into the eulogy depending on the account. Some accounts go so far as to say St. Mars wandered miserably through the region, begging forgiveness until St. Melaine deigned to grant it. St Mars is freed from the serpent coiling around him, but still having to do more penance, is stripped of his title of bishop, a rather harsh punishment showing this may indeed be an embellishment. According to Hamon's book, in remembrance of this miracle and the lesson it gave on Christian charity, Foulques Nerra and Hildegarde dedicated the Abbey to Our Lady of Charity. Hildegarde established the custom of distributing bread on the Tuesdays of Holy Week each year.

heaven; I adore the Supreme Priesthood of which the rod of Aaron was the symbol, I adore the High Priest par excellence, the priest according to the order of Melchizedek.

Also I admire without astonishment the so perfect conformity of Mary to the law of grace, her zeal to collect the smallest parcels of the divine manna which for the soul are the food of truth and justice: *Maria autem conservabat omnia verba haec, conferens in cord suo;* ("Mary kept all these words, pondering them in her heart," Luke 2:19). I finally admire in Mary that life of sacrifice which assures the merit of the priesthood.

In the Church I also see the law, the very word of Jesus, which is preserved there infallibly by the mouth of Peter; and the manna, the Bread of Life descended from heaven, the Body of Jesus present in the Eucharist; and the rod of the high priest, the Priesthood of Jesus Christ present in the person of His Vicar who holds in his hand the rod that corrects, and the sceptre that directs.

Christian, by Holy Communion, the law of God rests in you and abides there; manifest His presence by the regularity of your life. By Communion, the Heavenly Manna has descended into your heart: manifest Its action by living an entirely heavenly life. By Communion the Sovereign Priest associates you with His royal priesthood: be with Him (as He is) priest and victim at the same time, you will be one and the other, and by consecration you will be both, by the consecration of all that you are to the service and glory of the heavenly Father, and by the voluntary sacrifice of all that would oppose His good pleasure.

Notre Dame du Verger, or du Rocher

After the abbey of Ronceray we must mention that of Saint Aubin, famous for the chapel of Notre Dame du Verger. It was the work of the great St. Hilaire.[74] This distinguished Doctor of the Church, was born in Chéré in Anjou, and loved this beautiful region, his first homeland where the days of his childhood had passed. He wanted to endow Angers with a chapel of the Virgin. In this pious design, the year 356, he had the ground dug at the foot of a rock and he built an underground chapel there. Later, by the order of King Childebert, St. Germain of Paris founded in honour of St. Germain of Auxerre an abbey whose church was built above the chapel of Notre Dame du Rocher and consecrated also to the Mother of God. In this abbey the feast of the Assumption was solemnized for four days like those of Easter, of Christmas and of Pentecost, and since the general chapter of 1332, the feast of the Immaculate Conception was celebrated there according to the first class rite. However, the miracles performed when the body of St. Aubin, bishop of Angers, was transferred to this church, gave it, as well as the abbey, the name of this saint.[75] The levellers of 1793 destroyed the church

---

[74] St. Hilary of Poitiers (310-367 AD), Doctor of the Church and called the 'Hammer of the Arians' and the "Athanasius of the West".

[75] Fr. Marin de Boylesve's source, again the book by Hamon, says St. Hilary originally built the first structure to honour the Mother of God in imitation of the other basilicas built at the time which featured underground crypt chapels to either hide relics, or build a safe place where Christians could worship in peace and escape the malice of the pagans.

and part of the abbey.

༄༅

23 ~ The Ark, Council of Israel

(Num. 1: 50-54, 10: 35)

Placed in the middle of the camp, the holy Ark guarded Israel and Israel guarded the Ark.

Let us keep Mary in our heart, let us keep her well in thought, in prayer, and Mary will guard us.

When Moses, and after him the high priest, needed to consult God, he approached the holy ark and God answered.

Hamon states the place was first called Notre Dame du Verger, but also became known as Notre Dame du Rocher, Our Lady of the Rocks. (Hamon, 'Notre-Dame de France ou Histoire du culte de la Sainte Vierge en France, depuis l'origine du christianisme jusqu'à nos jours', 1864). According to other texts that do not site sources, St. Aubin was buried in a vault in the church of Saint-Pierre in Angers. A few years later, his body, according to Fortunatus himself (c. 53), was transported by Saint Germain of Paris, to a 'new basilica' either dedicated to St. Stephen or to St. Germain before it took the name of St. Aubin. This church was built on the order of King Childebert (511-558), and was built on the old structure of Notre Dame du Rocher. ('Les miracles posthumes de saint Aubin d'Angers', by Élisabeth Carpentier et Georges Pon, 2018.) Apparently, the vault the relics of St. Auben were placed was the original crypt from the earlier structure attributed to St. Hilary. St. Auben's chapel became famous for the numerous miracles of healing that happened there.

In difficulties, in anguish, let us have recourse to Mary; the response and help will not be long in coming.

Likewise, if the nations guard the Church, the Church will guard them, it will be their council. Woe to the philosopher, woe to the scientist, woe to the politician, woe to the legislator, who, wishing to separate reason from faith and the State from the Church, would refuse to consult faith and not listen to the Church! Assuredly reason suffices to recognize the first truths of science and the first principles of morality; but experience demonstrates that without the light of faith, without the supervision of the Church, reason seduced by passion and dominated by opinion does not take long to go astray when it comes to draw up the consequences and make the practical applications, and then woe to the peoples if those who direct them do not consult the Holy Ark, that is to say, the infallible Church of Jesus Christ!

Faithful Christian, by your example, as much and more than by your word, in the midst of the world you will be the advice and the light of those who doubt or who hesitate.

Notre Dame de Sous-Terre

On the hill of Levière[76] once stood a monastery of Benedictines. These monks placed a statue of the Blessed Virgin in an underground crypt. They came to honour her under the title of Notre Dame de Sous-Terre. Jean-sans-Terre while besieging Angers ruined the chapel and broke the statue (1205). Two centuries later (around 1400), Yolande, wife of Louis II, Count of Anjou, walking along the Levière coast and sitting on the height saw a rabbit come out of a bush which, pursued by dogs, came to take refuge on her knees. Suspecting in this fact some mysterious clue, the princess ordered the ground at the place occupied by the bush be dug up. A small vault was discovered in which was an image of the Virgin with the Infant Jesus in her arms, a glass lamp was suspended in front of the image. Yolande had a small oratory built in this place and the statue was placed there. A pilgrimage was established there. A little later the chapel of Notre

---

76 I.e. L'Esvière, in Angers.

Dame de Sous-Terre was rebuilt, and the statue was put there.[77] Then came the devastations of the Huguenots. The chapel was destroyed, but the statue was saved. In 1793, new destruction, and thanks to the zeal of pious people, new preservation of the statue which, in 1826, was deposited in the church of Saint-Laud. In 1849 it was stolen and dumped in the Maine. But fishermen caught her in their nets and she was carried back to Saint-Laud. Today it has been transferred to a chapel rebuilt in the place it once occupied. Among other miracles operated in the past at Notre Dame de Sous-Terre, we cite the healing of the Lord of Boylesve who, despairing of doctors, devoted himself to Notre Dame de Sous-Terre and vowed, if he was cured, to bring the shroud in which he was to be buried (as an offering). Immediately he returned to health.[78]

---

[77] This priory was given the double title Saint-Sauveur et de la Trinité de L'Esvière, and sometimes simply rendered the priory of l'Esvière. According to sources, Yolande restored the priory in 1429, and various additions were made over the centuries. The Revolutionaries wreaked havoc of course, the priory was closed in 1790 and sold as national property January 25, 1792 to the Department for the installation of a hospital for foundlings, the project of which did not come to fruition. The church was destroyed around 1845. Of the priory of Esvière, only the chapel of Notre-Dame-Sous-Terre and a few annex buildings remain. The chapel was restored in 1873 although damaged during WWII, the restored again in 1954. Also, the original priory chapel of Saint-Eutrope chapel still exists and is the seat of the parish of L'Esvière.

[78] Fr. de Boylesve found this information in Hamon's book, it is unusual he did not give more details as given by Hamon as this could be one of his own ancestors that was cured considering Fr Marin was from the Boylesve noble family and the last of the noble line. The miracle apparently happened between 1632-1650 when fourteen cures were

24 ~ The Ark in the Time of Combat

(Joshua 3 and 6)

On the day of a battle, the Ark when brought into the ranks of Israel, usually assured it victory.

The overflowing Jordan closes the entrance to the promised land. The Ark advances, carried on the shoulders of the priests, immediately the river suspends its course and Israel passes.

Jericho stand in opposition with its ramparts; the Ark is carried by the priests around the proud city, and on the seventh day, on the seventh turn, its walls crumble.

In the day of combat, either against error and sophism, or against passion and vice, the Church is with us, the Church precedes us and directs us; let us follow it by faith and by obedience, and we will see the river of error and passion stopping to give us passage; we will see the ramparts of Jericho, the gates of hell, the high and great powers of this world crumble to leave us the empire, empire over sin, empire over human respect, empire over the flesh, empire over ourselves, empire over souls.

---

recorded, for the 'Lord Boislève' is listed as one of the recipient of these cures. Dying of pleurisy, in a raging fever to the point he could no longer speak and having lost the use of his senses, he was beyond the skill of the doctors. Obviously he had deteriorated to the point the shroud was prepared, for in desperation he promised Our Lady of Sous-terre that if he was cured, he would present it to her. Immediately after making this vow, he was cured.

The Ark before the walls of Jericho

In turn, you will be the strength of the weak and the terror of the wicked. In front of you, as in front of the Ark, they will see the waves stop and the ramparts crumble; they will see passions recede and obstacles fall.

Notre Dame de Fontevrault

On the borders of Anjou and Poitou there was once a vast forest. A brigand, famous under the name of Evrault, had established his lair there near a fountain which from his name was called Fontevrault (Fons Evraldi).[79] Around the year 1095 Robert d'Arbrisselle founded in this solitary place a religious order of both sexes in which men, in imitation of the submission to Jesus, and also of St. John to Our Lady, made a vow of obedience to the abbess who was superior of the entire order.[80] The magnificent church of this monastery was consecrated to the Blessed Virgin by Pope Callixtus II in 1119. Ehrni II and Richard the Lionheart wanted to be buried there. Today this splendid abbey serves as a central prison.[81]

---

79 Also spelled Fontevraud.
80 Note: Hamon only mentions the men submitted in obedience in imitation of Our Lord and also St. John, but without mentioning Our Lady. Fr. de Boylesve may have been attempting to explain why the men of the order would submit to an abbess and not an abbot.
81 The abbey church was the burial place of Henry II of England, his wife Eleanor of Aquitaine, and their son Richard I the Lion Heart. However, there is no remaining corporal presence of Henry, Eleanor, Richard, or the others on the site. Their remains were possibly destroyed during the French Revolution. Under Napoleon the buildings were turned into a

Notre Dame des Ardilliers

This sanctuary, one of the most famous in France for the great miracles that took place there, owes its origin to an image in stone of the Mother of God, which was venerated in the cave where it was hidden by a fervent religious of Saint-Florent named Absalon, who had been chased from his monastery by the Normans.[82] This statue was later exposed to the devotion of the people under a stone arch. It represented the Virgin seated, holding in her arms her dead Son, taken down from the cross. It was called Notre Dame des Ardilliers, because the ground in this place is clayey and the dialect of the country gives the clay the name of *ardille*. – A man who once tried to remove the statue was struck with immobility until he

---

prison until 1963 when it was given to the Ministry of Culture restoration work was commenced. Since 1975 it has hosted the Centre Culturel de l'Ouest and was opened to the public in 1985. Restoration of the abbey was completed in 2006.

82   In ancient times the fountain was once the place of pagan sacrifices. A monastery that had been founded by Charlemagne at Saumur was destroyed by the Normans and the one surviving monk retired to a cave near the spring of Ardilliers, a statue of Our Lady his sole remaining treasure from the monastery. A small statue discovered near the spring in 1454 is believed to be the one he carried. The miracles that occurred in connection with this image caused the erection of a small arch for it above the spring, the waters of which were found to have healing virtues. A chapel was built and dedicated in 1553 and grew as successive additions were made, notably by Cardinal Richelieu. The Oratorians were placed in charge (1614). During the Revolution the church was robbed of its treasures, but was not destroyed, and the image was left unharmed. The church was restored in 1849.

Altar at Notre Dame des Ardilliers

asked forgiveness from the Mother of God. – Three others having conceived the same project succeeded in loading it on their horses, but not being able to advance a step, they were obliged to put the image under the arch – Finally, a suitable sanctuary was erected. – Among the pilgrims to Notre Dame des Ardilliers we cite M. Olier who returned there several times, and the venerable Grignon de Montfort, (St-Louis Marie de Montfort, 1673-1716), founder of the Priests of the Holy Spirit and the Sisters of Wisdom. – A large number of Protestants have abjured their heresy at the feet of this image.

25 ~ The Ark among the Philistines

(1 Kings 4, 5, 6)

Carried by unworthy hands, the Ark was one day taken by the Philistines; but at its approach the idols fell, and the infidels were stricken with a dreadful disease.
Thus, always invincible Queen, Mary dominates in the midst of her enemies: *Dominare in medio inimicorum tuorum.* ("Rule thou in the midst of thy enemies" Psalm 109:2)
Invoke Mary, she will overthrow the idol of prejudice in your intelligence, the idol of passion in your heart.

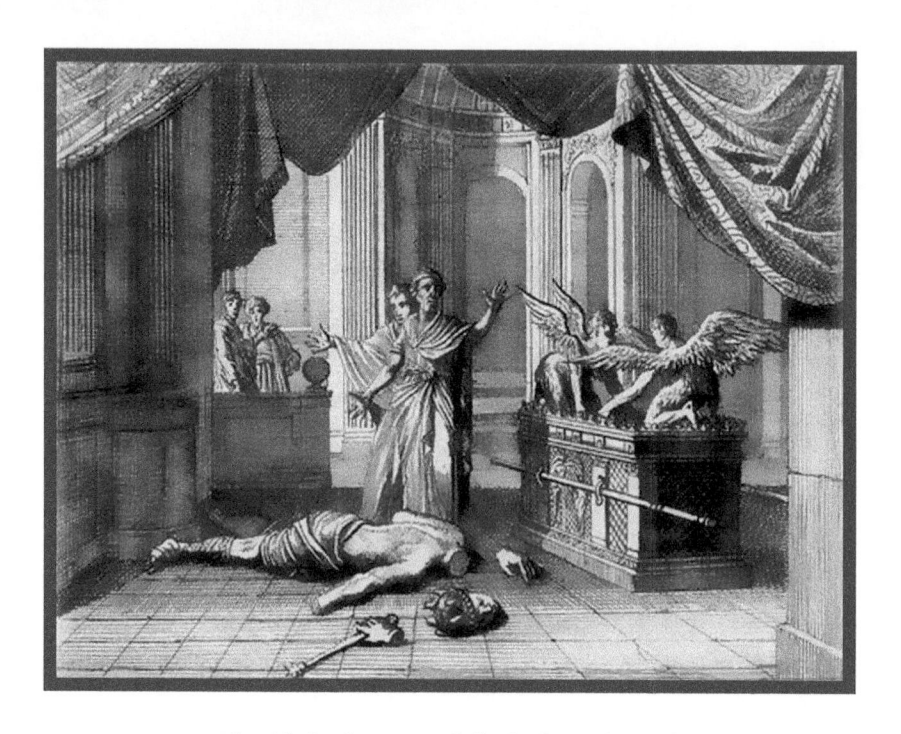

The idol of Dagon falls before the Ark

    Woe to the unworthy priest! By him the Church is delivered to ungodly powers. But he will share the fate of the guilty sons of the high priest Heli.

    Woe to the Philistines, woe to the impious, especially at the moment when believing they are triumphant, they seem to hold the Church under their sway. The Church was born to dominate. Free and sovereign everywhere, even if she were captive and chained, she must reign and triumph. Her presence alone topples and shatters the idols the world adores. Neither gold, nor iron, nor opulence, nor force can stand before her. For she too is strength, but spiritual strength, and this strength outweighs the strength of the world as much as spirit outweighs matter.

Be firm, Christian, and do not tremble. Were you surrounded by the impious and the libertines: the idols they adore will fall and break before you.

Notre Dame de Cunault

The canton of Gennes offers to the admiration of the pilgrims the church of Our Lady of Cunault. This name comes from the Latin word *cunae*, cradle, because in this sanctuary the Infant Jesus is honoured in the cradle and nursed by his Mother. The tradition attributes the foundation of this church to King Dagobert (630 AD).[83] Here was kept the ring that St. Joseph put on the finger of the Blessed Virgin during her wedding ceremony. This ring was of very pure gold, and enriched with a precious stone which was believed to be a very fine blue amethyst.

Cunault also had a rock crystal vial encased in silver, in which milk from the Blessed Virgin was kept.

Geoffrey, Count of Anjou, exempted the church of Cunault from all secular jurisdiction in the year when, with the help of God and of His Blessed Mother, he acquired the part of Normandy which is on this side of the Seine. *Actum est andegavis in anno quo, annuente Deo et sancta Matre ejus, partem Normann aequae est citra Sequanam acquisivimus,* (1143).

ஓ☙ଓ

---

[83] The monastery is reputed to have been founded by Saint Maxenceul, a disciple of Saint Martin of Tours. The abbey was sacked and destroyed during the French Revolution.

26 ~ The Ark, the Bethsamites and Oza

The Bethsamites cast a prying eye upon the Ark, they are stricken with death (1 Kings 6:19); Oza bears a reckless hand on it, he is struck dead. (2 Kings 6:7).

Do not seek to scrutinize the mysteries accomplished in Mary. Defend her glory assuredly, she is your Mother, she is your queen; but do not try to explain it: she is the masterpiece of the wisdom and power of God. Now, it is written: "He who gazes upon the majesty, will be crushed by the glory", of this supreme majesty. *Qui scrutator est majestatis, opprimetur a gloria.* ("As it is not good for a man to eat much honey, so he that is a searcher of majesty, shall be overwhelmed by glory," Proverbs 25:27)

Woe to the Bethsamites! Woe to Oza! Do not look, do not touch.

Look not: dispense with watching and examining the teaching of the Church or its government. You do not have the right.

Touch not: (but) I do not say to (not) strike, I even say to protect. Wise and powerful of the age, read her history. It will tell you what was the fate of kings, magistrates, ministers, councils and assemblies who dared to submit the acts of the Church, the bulls and decrees of her Pontiffs to their (secular) examination and to their placet, or raise their hand against either the people or even the things that belong to her. Protect, it is your duty, but without touching.[84]

---

[84] It appears Fr. de Boylesve was making a point about the dangers of indulging in an impertinent, over-curious probing into theology beyond our state in life and a defiant

Le Puy-Notre Dame[85]

In 996 King Robert, son of Hugues Capet, saw his crown threatened by a powerful lord named Berthold. He was a very feared giant because of his extraordinary strength. Queen Constance invited Geoffrey Grisegonelle, Count of Anjou, to fight this warrior, and, to excite his confidence, she presented him with a girdle of the Blessed Virgin which had once been sent from Constantinople to Charlemagne. Equipped with this belt Geoffrey advanced against Berthold as David once did against Goliath, he killed the giant and routed his army. For a reward, he asked for the precious belt that had been lent to him for the fight. This belt is made of linen gray wool fabric, with small silk nets.

Around the eleventh century William VI, Duke of

---

questioning against the dogmas regarding Mary challenging the teaching authority of the Church on the matter. We have a duty to learn about Mary, but to also know our place when doing so - what the Church declares regarding her we are to believe and have no right to question or oppose. Also, Our Lady will defend what is hers and will not have her glory taken from her, but we too have a duty to defend the Mother of God's honour as her subjects whenever it is attacked or maliciously questioned.

85   This sanctuary with the holy belt is situated in the Pays de Loire region and is different from the Le Puy mentioned in Ch. 17 with the statue of the Black Virgin. The sanctuary still has the relic of the belt as a local travel site says it is possible to attend the pilgrimage of the Holy Belt of the Virgin every Sunday after September 8.
https://www.france-voyage.com/events/le-puy-notre-dame-commune-17141.htm

Aquitaine, built at Puy Notre-Dame, in the canton of Montreuil, a church in honour of the Blessed Virgin with a monastery where he established religious of St. Benedict to preserve the belt of the Mother of God. The brilliance of the miracles wrought in this sanctuary gave it great celebrity.

In 1240 St. Louis came there with his brothers and all his court. Louis XI often made this pilgrimage. Charles VIII and Louis XIII also lived there.

During her first pregnancy, Anne of Austria had nine masses sung at Puy Notre Dame, and the sash was brought to her by two canons. The queen asked for the holy relic again on the 7th of August 1638, she was invested with it when on the 5th of September she gave birth to a son whom, out of gratitude she called Dieudonné, and whom France later named Louis-le-Grand. Two years later, in the month of September 1640, she again claimed the belt, and having put it on she gave birth to a second son who was Philippe, Duke of Orleans. In 1642 she went herself to Puy Notre Dame with the Dauphin and presented him to the canon who, the first time, had brought her the relic, she said to him: "Messire Christopher, here is one of the fruits of your belt."

At the time of the Revolution the church was devastated. A local man, named Guillon, mingled with the looters as if to take part in the booty and he stole the holy relic to save it. When the storm was over, he handed it over to the priest.

            ෩❀ര

27 ~ The Ark and its Blessings

(2 Kings 6: 10-12)

In the abode of virtuous Obededom, the Ark becomes a source of blessings.

Present in a heart, in a house, in a family, in a city, by the honours that are paid to her, by the prayers that are addressed to her, Mary does not cease to spread happiness there.

Happy the nations, happy the families who, respectful and docile, gratefully receive the teaching and direction of the infallible and immaculate Church. God will bless them, as He blessed the virtuous child of Israel who received the ark into his house.

Happy the cities, happy the families which possess in their bosom a faithful and fervent Christian! If he is treated there with the respect which his virtue deserves, he is for the family and for the whole city a continual blessing.

The Belt of the Blessed Virgin at Loches (1)[86]

The ancient collegiate church of Notre Dame du château de Loches, built by the Count of Anjou, Geoffrey Grisegonelle, and rebuilt almost entirely in

---

[86] (Original footnote in book.) (1) The dimensions of the Loaches Belt, (only 3 centimeters wide), suggests that the Count of Anjou reserved the main part for Anjou and that he detached only a fairly narrow strip of the precious relic for the church of his castle of Loches.

1160 by Thomas Pactius, prior of the Chapter, has become the parish church of St-Ours since 1802.

There is preserved a belt of the Blessed Virgin given by Count Geoffrey to his church of the Castle. Tradition and the archives of the former Chapter of Notre Dame agree that this insignia relic had been sent from Constantinople to the Emperor Charles the Bald, who died in 877 AD (others say to Charlemagne), and that from its translation to France until the year 978 (996, according to others), it was kept with honour in the royal chapel.

However, Geoffrey Grisegonelle, having agreed to fight alone against a German prince who disputed with the king of France his rights to the crown, the queen sent as a safeguard to the Count of Anjou the belt of the Blessed Virgin kept in the chapel of his palace. She recommended him to wear it during the fight, assuring him that the Virgin Mary to whom this Belt had belonged would bring him victory. That is what happened.

After Geoffrey's victory that assured them the tranquil possession of the throne, the king and queen gave him the precious relic, which he hastened to deposit in his church at the Château de Loches.

From that moment the holy relic was the object of universal veneration there. The history of the Collegiate has preserved for us the names of the kings and princes of royal blood who came to venerate it. Philippe Augustus, St. Louis IX, Philippe-le-Bel, John II, Charles VII, Louis XI, Louis XII, and Queen Anne of Brittany, Francis I and Charles V, Henry II and Catherine de Medici, Charles IX, Henry III, the grandson of Louis XIV. Philippe V, going to Spain to take possession of the throne there, came to the collegiate church, and they used their royal birthright

*Church of Saint-Ours de Loches
where the relic of the belt is kept*

to have exposed for veneration the belt of the Mother of God. Each year it was exposed to public veneration on May 3rd and the 15th of August; on those days the Christian people flocked to the Collegiate Church, and one often saw in its ranks persons illustrious by birth or holiness, such as Blessed Jeanne de Maillé. The rest of the year, the Belt was carefully locked in a double-doored cupboard, lined with iron and equipped with five locks.

The Belt of the Blessed Virgin is of a very fine, straw-coloured fabric,[87] the material of which is probably linen. It is 2 meters 10 c. long. Before the

---

87 Some accounts describe it a hazelnut colour.

Revolution it was kept in a rich vermeil reliquary, made on the model of the church of the Holy Sepulchre of Jerusalem. It rested on an agate of rare beauty enriched with gold and precious stones.

When the revolutionaries came to plunder the collegiate church, the rich reliquary which contained the Belt tempted their cupidity; so they stole it; but the holy relic was saved from their sacrilegious hands by Fr. Pierre-René Leduc.

In 1803, it was brought back to the Church of the Castle and solemnly recognized, the 7th of August, by the former canons and chaplains of the Collegiate.

In 1834, Mgr de Montblanc, archbishop of Tours, allowed it to be displayed, as in the past, to the veneration of the faithful.

It is now placed on a cushion of cloth of gold, to which it has been firmly fixed by fasteners bearing the archiepiscopal seal, and enclosed in a reliquary of gilded bronze, representing a Gothic church.

Public devotion to this belt has been preserved in Loches, and attracts a large crowd there on the days dedicated to its festivals. It has given rise to a custom which goes back to great antiquity: that of having blessed ribbons touch the relic, which are then worn with confidence in the protection of the Blessed Virgin. Young girls love to wear these ribbons on their First Communion and wedding day. There are several old Lochoise families that have ribbons that are more than two hundred years old.

Permission to print, Imprimatur, May 17, 1879

✠ CHARLES, arch. De Tours.

28 ~ The Ark in the Temple

In the Temple the place of the Ark was in the Holy of Holies where only the high priest could enter.

In heaven the place of Mary is at the right hand of the Holy of Holies, by her Son, the Eternal Priest: for on the day of the sacrifice she stood by the cross.

Finally, like the Ark of the Covenant, the Church has its marked place in the holy of holies; in Heaven, of which the Temple was the symbol, it will surround Jesus, His Divine Head and the veritable Holy of Holies.

And you, faithful soul, rise, rise again, rise from virtue to virtue; your place is in Heaven, near Jesus, the Holy of Holies, near Mary, the Queen of saints, holy ones: For it shall be given to the victor to sit in the very throne of the King of Glory: *Qui vicerit, dabo ei sedere mecum in throno meo.* (Apoc. 3:21)

Notre Dame de Pontron

At Pontron, in the parish of Louroux, there was formerly a sanctuary dedicated to Mary and famous in the region. The Angevin lords who went to the crusade preached by St. Bernard, came to put themselves under the protection of our Lady of Pontron and they prayed for her to bless their flags and their arms.

Notre Dame de Béhuart[88]

The canton of Saint-Georges has Notre Dame de Béhuart was built by Louis XI on the tip of a rock, on a small island in the middle of the Loire, which is two leagues from Angers. From the first centuries, there was a hermitage there with a chapel dedicated to the Virgin.[89] It was the meeting place for pilgrims from the region. Louis XI, when still dauphin, was crossing the Charente one day near Ruffec together with the king his father, his uncle Charles, who was the count of Maine, and Louis de Valory. The boat capsized and the four passengers fell into the river, the current of which at this place is very strong. Louis invoked Our Lady of Béhuart, and all four were thrown on the shore. Louis XI shared the testimonies of his gratitude between Béhuart in Anjou and Cléry in Orleans: he had a beautiful church built in Béhuart and raised that of Cléry.

Notre-Dame de Marillais

One kilometre from the church of Saint-Florent stands Notre-Dame de Marillais, one of the largest and most beautiful chapels in France. It is said that in this place Charlemagne won a great victory and that he attributed it to the help of Mary, saying: "Mary is there." From the Latin inscription: *Maria illic est*, the

---

88 Also spelled Notre Dame de Béhuard.
89 The statue was placed on the rock there by St. Maurille.

Sanctuary of Notre-Dame de Marillais

people would have made by alteration: Marillais. – Other etymologies are also given. – Formerly this pilgrimage was very famous; people came there from Germany itself and from England. On the 8th of September, the crowd was so great that more than a hundred oxen were needed to feed the multitude.[90]

ಸಿ ✿ ೞ

29 ~ The Interior Life of Mary

(Quoted from an unknown author.)

As Jesus Christ was the perfect and worthy adorer of God His Father; also Mary was the most perfect adorer and the most worthy imitator of her Son. She therefore of all pure creatures is the one who has honoured God most perfectly.

As long as she lived on earth, she never had the slightest attachment to any creature. Her heart always went to God with all the ardour of which she was capable, so that nothing in the world could ever weaken the tenderness of her love: loving all creatures; but loving them only in God and for God.

Her holy soul, united to the Heart of Jesus, was like a sacred temple where her God resided and where she contemplated and adored Him unceasingly.

---

[90] Strangely, Fr. Marin de Boylesve omits the detail that this was the location where it is said St. Maurille had his vision revealing the nativity date of Our Lady, September 8. (See Chapter 20, Mount Sinai - L'Angevine, fn. 63). The old chapel was replaced by a sanctuary built between 1890 and 1913 by the architect Beignet.

Recognizing her baseness and her nothingness, she thought herself incapable of worthily glorifying this supreme Majesty; and in this humility regarding her incapacity, she entreated Him to condescend to praise and glorify Himself therein through Jesus Christ her Son.

She never turned her mind and her heart away from the presence and sentiment of her God. When she carried her spirit towards this Eternal Being, her soul remained attached by a contemplation and a love which surpasses all the efforts and expressions of the human spirit.

Not being subject to the impressions of the senses, she received the celestial word and divine inspirations with such abundant plenitude that her soul, stripped of human sentiments, was lost, so to speak, in the bosom of the Divinity, and never was there a mind more in one with God.

The whole interior of her soul was therefore as if deified; and whoever could have seen this pure soul, would have seen the Divinity dwelling there as on a throne of holiness. Oh! Who could say how many divine secrets and profound mysteries were revealed to her in these sublime ecstasies, and what delights she experienced there? When one could unite all that there can be of lights, pleasures and charms in the world; all this compared to what Mary felt would be only darkness and bitterness.

Exempt from original sin from the first moment of her conception, she never experienced, as we do, the rebellion of any passion. This privilege was due to her dignity and reserved for her alone. It was not right that she who was to be the Mother of God, was for a single moment the slave of the demon; nor that the temple which Holiness and Eternal Wisdom had chosen was

Statue de Notre-Dame-du-Chef-du-Pont
in the church of Saint-Thomas de La Flèche

ever stained with the slightest spot; nor finally that she who was to crush the head of the serpent and destroy the reign of Satan, was for a single moment infected with his venom, nor submitted to his empire.

(*Anonymous author*)

Notre Dame à la Flèche

In a part of Anjou which today is part of the diocese of Le Mans, at the entrance to a bridge over the Loir, there once stood a modest chapel called Notre-Dame-du-Chef-du-Pont. Many miracles first attracted pilgrims to this place, then inhabitants. Such is the origin of the city of La Flèche. The old sanctuary of Mary is today a side chapel of the old Carmelite church.

At the beginning of the 17th century, Henri IV established a college of Jesuits at La Flèche and he donated to them a statuette, about ten inches high, which represented the Virgin carrying the Divine Infant on her left arm and a sceptre in the right hand. Four congregations of the Blessed Virgin were established in the college, and embraced all classes of society: one, of the Conception, for externs; the other, of the Assumption, for interns; the third, of the Purification, for the notables; the fourth, of the Nativity, for the workers and the merchants. Then, the Fathers added to the oratory of Saint-Barthélemy a new sanctuary where they placed a statue of the Blessed Virgin, under the name of Our Lady of Virtues. This pilgrimage is still flourishing.[91]

---

91   The statue is now called Notre-Dame-du-Chef-du-Pont

30 ~ The Virtues of Mary

Although Mary was always united to God within by a continual contemplation which raised her above herself, she was none the less occupied abroad regulating all her conduct and in fulfilling all her duties through judicious and holy actions. But, she filled them with such profound humility, with such tender devotion, with such lively faith, with such perfect confidence, with such ardent love and with such pure and holy intentions that her smallest actions were more precious before God than those of all the saints.

By her humility she deserved to be elevated to the dignity of Mother of God. Humility so sincere that, at the moment when the Angel announced to her that she was full of grace and that she would be Mother of Jesus, she recognized herself so unworthy of this elevation that she hardly thought herself worthy of being the smallest of the servants of God. Humility so great that she only tremblingly received the graces of God, and that she never dared to ask for any light, or knowledge, or favour, except according to the designs and the order of God

Her faith was so lively and so submissive that, although she had an understanding of the mysteries, she never dared to reason about them, nor to penetrate them further than God commanded. She had a sovereign respect for all that was consecrated to God and for all that concerned His worship. She never

---

in reference to the old chapel from which it comes. It has been kept in the Saint-Thomas church since 1860 and listed since 1908.

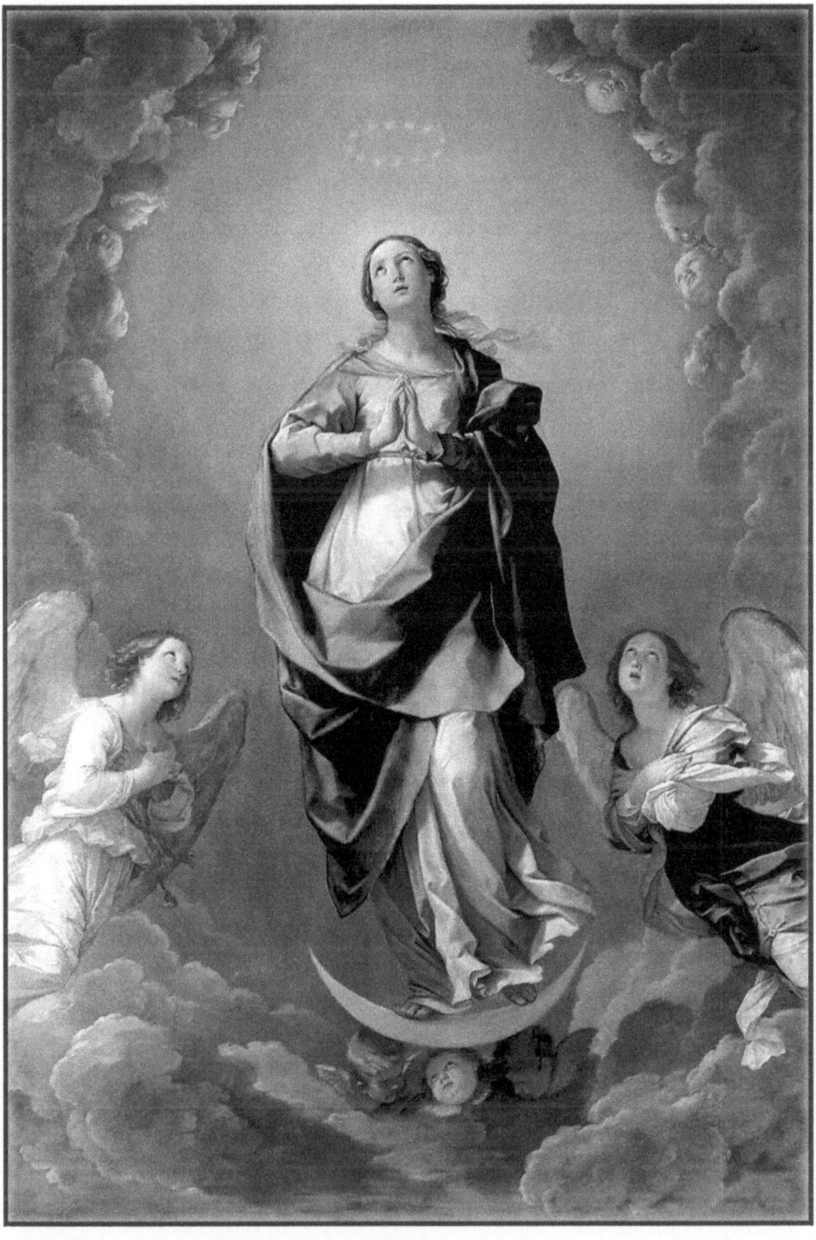

entered the Temple except with a holy trembling, there to annihilate herself before the Majesty of the Most High. In her prayers, she offered herself to God with all her powers, consecrating to Him all that depended on her. She asked God, through Jesus Christ her Son, her favours and her mercy for others; but as for her, recognizing herself unworthy of any grace, she only asked God to deign to accomplish His always adorable designs for her.

When she heard the Divine Word (even in the simplest terms) it was always in a spirit of faith, impressing what she heard more and more on her heart with an infinite desire to accomplish it down to the smallest points.

Animated by this faith, the most perfect that has ever been, in all creatures she looked only to God, especially in those who were invested with the sacred character. In all the different events of life, happy or unfortunate, she reported everything to God, adoring the wisdom and equity of His divine guidance in everything that happened.

Her confidence in God was so firm that in the harshest trials through which she passed, and during the most annoying contradictions, her courage was always unshakable and her heart always united and submitted to God, expecting everything from Him alone.

Her love for God was so ardent that she alone loved Him more than all the saints together. She experienced incredible pain during her life; but the most sensitive thing was to see that God was not loved, that He was unknown and offended; so that her life (in spite of the peace which her holy soul enjoyed) was a life of tears and groans, and she would have suffered death a thousand times to prevent a single venial sin.

One cannot understand how far she bore the spirit of penance. When she considered the humiliations and the sufferings to which Jesus Christ her Son had given Himself up to atone for the sins of the world, she would have liked to place herself below nothingness, giving herself up to self-contempt, to tears and to the bitterest pain. And far from asking for the end of her labours and her pains, she offered herself with all her heart; uniting herself as a victim of atonement, to the suffering Jesus Christ.

Her patience was the most courageous: as she was the most conformed to Jesus Christ, she also had the biggest share of His cross! For after Jesus, no one has ever been more afflicted or more persecuted than Mary. The memory of the admirable patience with which her Son, that innocent Victim, had endured without complaint, the torments of His Passion made such a vivid impression on Mary that she embraced all occasions of suffering with ardour and wanted to endure every ill imaginable.

(Anonymous)

Louis XIII and the Immaculate Conception

Letter of Louis XIII to Pope Urban VIII

"Most Holy Father, although we know that only Your Holiness (has the authority to declare what is acceptable) regarding piety and the veneration of saints and especially the glorious Virgin, we have believed it to be our duty to testify what is our devotion to the Mother of God, if not procuring a final decision on her Immaculate Conception, leaving it to prudence and what the Holy Spirit will dictate to be believed in the Church: at least pleading with Your Holiness with all the extent of our affection, to order that through all Christendom her feast under the title of the Immaculate Conception be solemnized, as it is already celebrated by all our kingdom."

Signed: Louis.

Following this letter, the 'Semaine Catholique de Toulouse' has published this note:

"This letter was delivered to Pope Urban VIII by the ambassador of France to Rome.
It is dated November 24, 1624. It was the year after the promotion of this pope to the sovereign pontificate.
A very esteemed writer from Toulouse, who wishes to honour us with his benevolence, discovered this document in the 'Vieilles archives de la guerre', (Vol. XII, item 83), and condescended to communicate it to us.
Good King Louis XIII's request was not granted. Pope Urban VIII, in fixing the ecclesiastical calendar, did not consider it appropriate to place among the holidays that of the Immaculate Conception."[92]

---

[92] Apparently, Fr. de Boylesve wished to show as an example that even though the request was not granted then, from historical hindsight in can be seen that devotion to the Mother of God in France was so great it was ahead of its time in piously recognizing what would eventually be declared a dogma of faith.

31 ~ Continuation of the Virtues of Mary

Her charity for her neighbour was the most effective and the most tender. Doing good to all, she never caused pain or harm to anyone, and never complained of anyone, whatever wrong or affront that was done to her: sincerely loving everyone, and all her enemies, in the Heart of Jesus.

Her purity was so admirable that she blushed and was disturbed at the sight of an Angel who appeared to her in the form of a young man, and that she would have preferred not to be Mother of God, than to cease to be a Virgin.[93] If she was the most beautiful of all women, she was also the most modest of all Virgins: modesty so great that even the Angels revered her, and that no mortal has ever dared to look her in the face without being imbued with a respect that amounted to veneration, so august and divine was the Majesty of the Spirit of God which shone upon her.

Her prudence was incomparable: never doing, or

---

[93] I.e. if she had to choose between these two great honours, virginity or the Divine Motherhood, she would choose the virtue of virginal purity over the honour of becoming the Mother of God. We also note Our Lady questioned the angel and tested him regarding keeping her purity, she had made a vow of virginity, and she knew God would not expect her to retract this vow. If he had said anything that would have been contrary to her vow, she would have rejected it as not coming from God. She accepted the Divine Motherhood when the angel confirmed her virginity would not be touched and she would conceive by the power of the Holy Spirit. She then replied, "Let it be done unto me, according to *thy* word,', i.e. exactly in the manner as he had said.

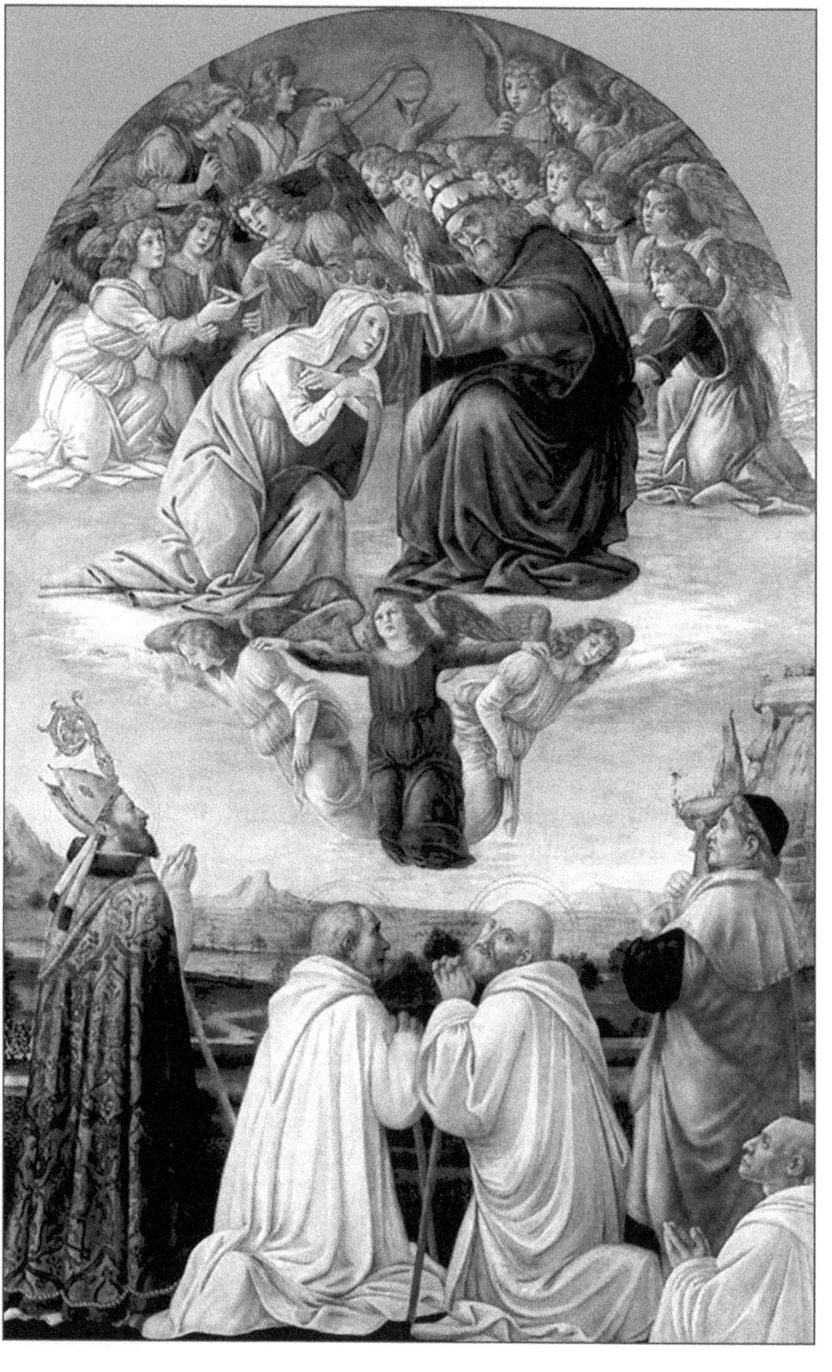

omitting or saying anything but what was proper. Before speaking, she examined what could come from it for the glory of God and for the edification of her neighbour. With such precautions she said in a few words what she had to say, and discreetly avoided worldly company.

Her detachment was so complete and her views so purified that she performed all her actions, even the smallest, with the noblest and most holy sentiments. Never in drinking, in eating, in her conversations, nor even in her acts of virtue did she seek her own satisfaction. God alone was the end, as He was the principle of all conduct; the intention of pleasing Him determined and regulated every moment of her life.

Her very sleep was a homage rendered to her Creator by the care she took to consecrate it to Him; and during her rest, which was short, she never had any other ideas than ideas of holiness, for her spirit always turned towards God. In a word, there was never in the soul of the Blessed Virgin, in her imagination and in her memory, any illusion or any vain thought. In hers words, there was never anything useless and unregulated. Never in all her conduct, in any action, or in her heart, was there any movement that was not holy and of the spirit of God.

The Most Holy Trinity always surrounded her to protect and sanctify her more and more. The Father viewed her as His Daughter; the Son loved her as His Mother; the Holy Spirit cherished her as His Spouse, and the Angels revered her as their Queen. Such is the idea that we can have of the interior life and the public life of the Blessed Virgin.

She is, after Jesus Christ, our most perfect model - let us therefore imitate her virtues. Her name, after that of JESUS, is the holiest of all names, let us invoke her with respect. After Jesus her Son, she is our mediator, our consolation, our hope and our life, so let us turn to her with confidence. St. Bernard says,"One can only go to the Heavenly Father through the Son, and one can only go to the Son through the Mother." Let us therefore go to Mary, and say to her often with the Church: 'O Mary, our Advocate! Cast upon us your glance of mercy: O sweet! O tender! O pious Mother! Let us see your adorable Son one day.' *Eia ergo, Advocata nostra! Illos tus misericordes oculos ad nos converte: Et Jesusm, benedictum fructum ventris tui, nobis post hoc exilium ostende. O clemens! Oh pia! O sweet Virgo Maria!*

(Anonymous).

Letter of Louis XIV on the Subject of the Immaculate Conception

King Louis XIV was happier than his pious and worthy father. In 1657, he addressed a similar petition to Pope Alexander VII, who responded favourably. It was on the occasion of the Brief of June 15, 1657 which, according to the wish of the king, declared by precept the feast of the Immaculate Conception, that Louis XIV addressed to the bishop of La Rochelle the following letter which we transcribe giving the spelling in use today:

"Msgr. The Bishop of Mailleraye. – In inheriting the crown which has been worn for many centuries by my predecessor kings, from whose blood I am descended, I have also been heir to their piety and devotion; so that if they had not already deserved the title of Most Christian Kings and defenders of our Mother the Holy Church, I would not dare to promise myself to acquire it. Several of them, namely the very Christian late king, my very honoured lord and father, of immortal memory, having had a very special devotion to the Most Blessed Mother of God, the Virgin Mary, and I, following their example, having recommended to her our affairs, I have often felt her protection, and how efficacious her prayers were before her Son; which having resolved to recognize by making her rendered in my empire an honour which marked my gratitude, and being moreover informed that the feast which the Church celebrates of her Immaculate Conception was not a precept, and that in several bishoprics it was not unemployed, I had recourse to our Holy Father Pope Alexander VII, now filling the chair of Saint Peter, to obtain that he issue a decree ordering all the bishops and archbishops whose dioceses are situated within the extent of my kingdoms, countries, lands, lordships of my obedience, to cause to be published in all places where spiritual jurisdiction extends, that henceforth the feast of the Immaculate Conception would be celebrated, a day of rest, and feted.

And His Holiness having had the pleasure of granting my request, as you will see from the copy of the Brief which he wrote to me which I send to you, I add my prayer to the liberty that he leaves you that what contained therein be religiously observed, trusting me further upon your care to cause my intelligence to be followed, to which I promise myself, by your zeal and devotion to the Blessed Virgin, which you will abide by and forget not to make those you commit to announce the word of God the day of the feast understand that you must ask the Divine Majesty to enlighten me on the things that are to be done for His glory and for His service, and gives me the strength, as has already done for my will, to execute and accomplish them.

I pray to Him from whom all good proceeds to have you in His holy keeping.

Written the 27th of October 1657.

LOUIS.

As a result of the same Brief, the vicars general of Toulouse, in the absence of Bishop de Marca, issued the following ordinance, which testifies to the ancient devotion of France to the Immaculate Conception:

"To all, abbots, provosts, deans, chapters, archpriests, parish priests and other priests in charge of souls in this present diocese, greetings.

The piety of our kings, since they embraced the Christian faith, has been so great towards the Blessed Virgin, that they have always had particular confidence in her intercessions, to the extent they put their crowns and everything of their kingdom under the protection of such a great Queen, who has begotten the King of all monarchs. This is the reason why they gave her all the honours that they could reasonably attribute to her, believing even to succeed more easily in better deserving the title of 'Very Christian Kings' by glorifying Our Lord Jesus Christ with a particular honour that they wanted to do towards His Mother.

For this effect, the feast of the Immaculate Conception had been accustomed to be observed in this kingdom for a long time up until the Constitution which Urban VIII made touching the observance of the feasts of precept, in the number of which he did not include it.

But the king, who does not want to fall from the piety of his predecessors, and who particularly wishes to imitate that of the late king, his father, of immortal memory, towards the Blessed Mother of God, having felt moreover powerful effects of his protection and felt how efficacious her prayers are to her Son, obtained a decree from our Holy Father Pope Alexander VII, now filling the pulpit of Saint Peter, whereby His Holiness, approving His Majesty's devotion to the Blessed Virgin and willing to satisfy his desires, removed the impediment which the constitution of Pope Urban brought to the customary observance of the feast of the Conception of Our Lady, and, in so doing, left the Church of France free to continue the possession in which it was to keep it as a feast of precept.

This is why, by virtue of the said decree, following the order which we have received from Mgr the Archbishop, and wishing to second the pious intentions of His Majesty and to continue the custom which this diocese had of observing it before the aforesaid constitution, we do hereby command you to cause to be observed, celebrated and feted henceforth, each year, the said feast of the Conception of the Virgin Mother of God, commencing on the eighth of the month of December following, on which day it falls, and continuing on similar days in subsequent years, etc.

Appendix One

The Brown Scapular of Our Lady of Mount Carmel

A Brief History of the Carmelites

In the Old Testament, the ancient prophets had devout followers who joined communities or 'schools', called 'Schools of the Prophets', which were a prefigurement of what would be religious communities today.

In the early centuries, a Christian community in the spirit of Elias the prophet founded an order on Mt. Carmel, the mountain where Elias battled with the pagan priests of Baal and where heavenly fire came and consumed his sacrifice. It is also where he had a vision of Our Lady, the promised Woman who would crush the head of the serpent. In the same spirit of Elias the habit of the early Christian order was brown like the camel hair he wore, and, the order was dedicated to Our Lady. They lived a meditative life there for centuries, until the Muslim Saracens began their bloody persecutions. Many were martyred, others fled to various regions such as Sicily, France and England, as well as other parts of Europe.

However, they still felt the sting of persecution and misunderstanding from the ecclesiastical authorities in the countries they fled to. The newcomers were perceived as a 'new order' and

Saint Simon Stock Receiving the Holy Scapular

therefore looked upon with suspicion when in fact the order was not new, while those who knew differently believed the spirituality of the meditative order was not compatible in other Christian countries once they had left their territory of Carmel, that basically, there was no room or need for such an order outside Mt. Carmel.

St. Simon Stock and the Revelation of the Scapular

St. Simon was born in Kent, England c. 1165. From an early age he felt the call to become a hermit and so when he was twelve he left home and lived an austere life in the woods, his home a hollowed out tree trunk, his food the wild herbs he could find. He was one of the first aspirants to enter the Carmelite order upon its arrival at Kent, no doubt the contemplative and austere life of the order attracted him. His reputation for sanctity spread in the order, and he was elected the first Prior-General of the Carmelites in the West in 1245.

However, as General of the Order of the "Brothers of the Blessed Virgin Mary", he was grieved by the bitter opposition against them, from the heartbreaking persecutions launched by the Saracens in the East, to the bitter prejudices they faced in the West. He defended the order against the unjust attacks, praying to Our Lady and practising austere penances for help. Then during a night vigil on July 16, 1251 he ardently prayed: "Flower of Carmel, Blossoming Vine, Brightness of Heaven, Solitary Virgin Mother, though without knowledge of man yet a meek

Mother, grant special favour to the Carmelites, O Star of the Sea."

His prayer was answered. Our Lady appeared with a heavenly retinue, and holding the habit of their order, the scapular, she offered it to him and said: "Beloved son, receive this scapular of your Order, token of my confraternity, as a guarantee of the privilege which I have obtained for you and all Carmelites. Whosoever shall die wearing it shall not suffer eternal fire. It is a sign of salvation, a safeguard in perils, a covenant of peace, a token of my special protection until the end of time."

The Blessed Virgin then advised him to appeal to the Pope to obtain assistance in their troubles.

Therefore, the Brown Scapular is a special sign of Our Lady's protection, and that her intercession will save those who wear it from eternal fire, that is, obtain for that soul the grace of final perseverance, and protection from many spiritual and also temporal dangers.

The Addition of the Sabbatine Privilege.

According to the Bull of Pope John XXII, the Blessed Virgin appeared to him and gave an additional promise to those who wear the Brown Scapular, saying, "I, the Mother of Grace, shall descend on the Saturday after their death and whomsoever I shall find in purgatory I shall free so that I may lead them to the holy mountain of life everlasting."

However Our Lady gave certain requirements that must be followed to obtain the Sabbatine Privilege.

1. Wear the Brown Scapular continuously. (One must be formally enrolled.)

2. Observe chastity according to one's state in life (married /single).

3. Recite daily the Little Office of the Blessed Virgin, OR Observe the fasts of the Church together with abstaining from meat on Wednesdays and Saturdays, OR with the permission of a priest, say five decades of Our Lady's Most Holy Rosary OR, with the permission of a priest substitute some other good work.

Questions and Answers about the Brown Scapular

What are the conditions for gaining the Our Lady's promise of the Brown Scapular?

1.) To observe exactly what has been prescribed regarding material, colour, and shape of the Scapular, that is it must be brown 100% woven sheep's wool in a rectangular shape. (Although black is also permitted.) The wool must be woven, it cannot be of a smashed felt with the fibres unwoven, (note: this sounds confusing, but felted wool is fine, which is woven wool fuzzed up and looks like felt, but it is woven). The scapular cannot be made of any other cloth. Other types of cloth are strictly forbidden. The straps, however, can be of cloth or even chains, but the main rectangular pieces of the cloth must be woven sheep wool. The shape must be rectangular or square, it cannot be oval, round, or polygonal. There can be a pious holy image on the scapular, such as Our Lady of Mt. Carmel or the Carmelite shield. However, the picture should not completely cover the brown, there should be a plentiful brown edge left so the scapular can be recognised for what it is. In other words, the brown (or black) wool must predominate the scapular.

2.) To be enrolled in the Scapular confraternity by a priest.

3.) To wear it continually.

Please note that there are no special prayers or good works that are necessary to receive the promise of salvation from eternal fire. The Scapular is a silent prayer that shows a person's complete consecration and dedication to the Blessed Virgin Mary. The Scapular is a devotion whereby we venerate Her, love Her, and trust in Her protection, and we tell Her these things every moment of the day by simply wearing the Brown Scapular.

However, for the Sabbatine privilege, see the requirements above.

Who may be invested in the Brown Scapular?

All the Catholic faithful should be enrolled. It is customary for children to be enrolled after their First

Holy Communion, but even infants can be invested.

How do I enrol in the Brown Scapular?

Any priest can enrol or invest you in the Brown Scapular. There is a special formula of investiture that the priest performs. The formula is included in the next section after the Questions and Answers.

Who can enrol me in the Brown Scapular?

Any Catholic priest can enrol you. It was once customary that only the Carmelite Fathers were permitted to enrol the lay faithful, and special permission was needed for any other priest to perform the ceremony. However, this devotion has spread so far and wide throughout the Catholic world that now the Church has given permission to all priests to invest the faithful in the Brown Scapular.

What is the Confraternity of the Brown Scapular?

Once invested in the Scapular a person automatically becomes a member of the Confraternity of the Brown Scapular. What is meant by the Confraternity is that having been enrolled in the Scapular, you belong to a spiritual family whereby you have the privilege of being affiliated with the Carmelite Order, participating in the merits of the Carmelite Fathers and Religious in life and in death, as well as receiving the promises of Our Lady through the

Scapular. Although at one time it was customary to inscribe one's name in the Confraternity Register (the parish priest would do this for all those he enrolled by sending the names to a Carmelite convent where the Confraternity was canonically erected), it is no longer the practice to do so. Part of the reason for this is that the Scapular has become, thanks be to God, such a universal sacramental and devotion that the Church has taken away this obligation upon the lay faithful. It is sufficient to be invested in the Scapular to be a member of the Confraternity.

How do I enrol in the Confraternity?

By being invested in the Brown Scapular by a priest.

Can an ordained deacon enrol a person in the Brown Scapular?

No, an ordained deacon cannot enrol a person in the Scapular. Only an ordained priest of the Catholic Church can perform the investiture.

How must I wear the Scapular in order to receive its benefits?

You must wear it over the shoulders so that one part hangs over your chest and the other side hangs over the back. Both parts cannot be carried in the front or the back, otherwise, the wearer runs the risk of not receiving the promise.

May the Scapular be fastened or pinned to my clothing?

The Scapular must hang over the shoulders with one side hanging in the front and the other side hanging in the back. However, one may sew or pin the scapular to an undergarment to hold it in place or to keep it from rising about one's neck.

What if I'm allergic to wool?

If one has a serious allergy to wool or has irritation of the skin, one can wear the wool scapular over one's clothing, encase the wool scapular in plastic, or wear the Scapular Medal with an image of the Sacred Heart on one side and an image of Our Lady on the other side. (Please see the question about the Scapular Medal).

Does the Scapular have to be touching the skin?

No, it may be worn over or under any part of the clothing.

May one wear a different colour of the Scapular?

Different colour Scapulars do exist as sacramentals in the Church for other devotions, such as the Red Scapular in honour of Our Lord's Passion. However, the Brown Scapular that the lay faithful wear is a miniature of the Carmelite Religious Habit, and since that Habit is brown in colour, it has always been regarded as the proper colour for the Scapular. However, black wool is permissible.

Must I always wear the Scapular or may I take it off?

In order to receive the promise, the Scapular must always be worn. We must understand that by wearing the Scapular we show our consecration and devotion to the Blessed Virgin. Our Blessed Mother cannot be pleased in any one who out of vanity or fear takes it off whenever it is not convenient to wear it. By wearing it we make an open profession of our faith, confidence, and love of Her.

But, may I take my Scapular off to bathe?

Yes.

May I wear a Scapular Medal as a replacement for my Scapular?

No, the medal was not meant to be a regular replacement. However, St. Pius X and subsequent Popes, have declared that in <u>necessary cases such as in foreign or tropical climate missions</u>, the Scapular Medal with an image of the Sacred Heart on one side and an image of Our Lady on the other side may be worn instead of the wool Scapular, <u>this is usually due to the scarcity of sheep's wool in those countries, and is *not meant to be the norm.*</u>

The Scapular Medal can also be worn in case of <u>*real necessity or for very serious reasons,*</u> such as an allergy to wool. <u>But if the Scapular Medal is worn for insufficient reason, such as vanity or convenience, the wearer runs the risk of not receiving the benefit of the Scapular promise.</u> It is important to remember that the small Scapular worn by the lay faithful is meant to be a miniature version of what the Carmelites wear as part of their Religious Habit, which is never substituted for anything else.

If I need a new Scapular, do I need to be re-invested?

No. If your Scapular has worn out or has broken, you only need to get another one and start wearing it. The blessing and investiture is still valid for the new Scapular, since the blessing is predominately given to the *person* who is invested in the Scapular.

What are the indulgences granted to those who devoutly wear the Scapular?

1. A plenary indulgence on the day of receiving the Scapular. Conditions: Confession and Communion.

2. Plenary indulgence at the moment of death. Conditions: Confession, Communion, and devout invocation with the lips, or at least with the heart, of the Holy Name of Jesus.

3. Reciting the Office of the Blessed Virgin Mary devoutly – 100 days indulgence.

4. Each time the Scapular is kissed – 500 days indulgence.

THE INVESTITURE CEREMONY
(In Latin and English)

In Latin

Priest: Ostende nobis Domine misericordiam tuam.

Respondent: Et salutare tuum da nobis.

V. - Domine exaudi orationem meum.

R - Et clamor meus ad te veniat.

V. - Dominus vobiscum.

R - Et cum spiritu tuo.

V. - Oremus. Domine Jesu Christe, humani generis Salvator, hunc habitum, quem propter tuum tuaeque Genitricis Virginis Mariae de Monte Carmelo, Amorem servus tuus devote est delaturus, dextera tua sancti ✠ fica, tu eadem Genitrice tua intercedente, ab hoste maligno defensus in tua gratia usque ad mortem perseveret: Qui vivis et regnas in saecula saeculorum. Amen.

(The Priest blesses the scapular with holy water and the person(s) being enrolled. He then invests that person(s), saying:)

V. - Accipite hunc, habitum benedictum

precantes sanctissima Virginem, ut ejus meritis illum perferatis sine macula, et vos ab omni adversitate defendat, atque advitam perducat aeternam. Amen.

(After the investiture, the priest continues with the following prayers):

V. - Ego, ex potestate mihi concessa, recipio vos ad participationem, omnium bonorum spiritualium, qua, cooperante misericordia Jesu Christi, a Religiosa de Monte Carmelo peraguntur. In Nomine Patris ✠ et Filii ✠ et Spiritus Sancti. ✠ Amen.

Benedicat ✠ vos Conditor caeli at terrae, Deus omnipotens, qui vos cooptare dignatus est in Confraternitatem Beatae Mariae Virginis de Monte Carmelo: quam exoramus, ut in hore obitus vestri conterat caput serpentis antiqui, atque palmam et coronam sempiternae hereditatis tandem consequamini. Per Christum Dominum nostrum.

R - Amen.

(The priest again sprinkles the person(s) enrolled with holy water.)

(End of the Investiture ceremony.)

English

Priest: Show us, O Lord, Thy mercy.

Respondent: And grant us Thy salvation.

P - Lord, hear my prayer.

R - And let my cry come unto Thee.

P - The Lord be with you.

R - And with your Spirit.

P - Lord Jesus Christ, Saviour of the human race, sanctify ✠ by Thy power these scapulars, which for love of Thee and for love of Our Lady of Mount Carmel, Thy servants will wear devoutly, so that through the intercession of the same Virgin Mary, Mother of God, and protected against the evil spirit, they persevere until death in Thy grace. Thou who livest and reignest world without end. Amen.

(The Priest blesses the scapular with holy water and the person(s) being enrolled. He then invests that person(s), saying:)

P - Receive this blessed scapular and beseech the Blessed Virgin that through Her merits, you may wear it without stain. May it defend you against all adversity and accompany you to eternal life. Amen.

(After the investiture, the priest continues with the prayers:)

P - I, by the power vested in me, admit you to participate in all the spiritual benefits obtained through the mercy of Jesus Christ by the Religious Order of Mount Carmel. In the name of the Father ✠ and of the Son ✠ and of the Holy Ghost. ✠ Amen.

May God Almighty, the Creator of Heaven and earth, bless ✠ you, He who has deigned to join you to the Confraternity of the Blessed Virgin of Mount Carmel; we beseech Her to crush the head of the ancient serpent so that you may enter into possession of your eternal heritage through Christ our Lord.

R – Amen.

(Once more, the priest sprinkles the person(s) enrolled with holy water.)

Appendix Two

The Blue Scapular of the Immaculate Conception

The Story of the Scapular

Consecrated by her parents to Virgin Mary's Immaculate Conception, Ven. Ursula Benincasa (1547-1618), spent part of her youth and adult life as a hermit in the region of Saint Elmo, Naples. In 1583, she founded the Congregation of the Oblates of the Immaculate Conception of the Most Blessed Virgin Mary. She also founded the Hermitage of the Contemplative Nuns of the Immaculate Conception. The rule of both communities was approved by Pope Gregory XV on April 7, 1623. , Pope Pius VI recognized the heroic virtues of Ursula, and proclaimed her Venerable on August 7, 1793

In 1617 in Naples, on the Feast of the Presentation of the Lord, having received Holy Communion, Ven. Ursula had a vision of the Blessed Mother clothed in a white garment over which she wore another garment of azure blue. In her arms, Mary held the Infant Jesus. Our Lady was surrounded by many persons all similarly attired. The Blessed Mother spoke to Ursula in these words:

"Cease weeping, Ursula, and turn your sighs into heartfelt joy. Listen closely to what Jesus, whom I am holding in my lap, will say to you."

Jesus then appeared to Ven. Benincasa and promised special favours for her religious order. She then begged Jesus for the same graces to such people who, living in the world, would have a special devotion to the Immaculate Conception, observe chastity according to their station in life, and wear a small blue scapular. Jesus granted her petition. As a sign that her prayer was heard, Jesus showed Ursula in a vision a multitude of angels distributing scapulars all over the world and she began to make small blue scapulars. One part bears the image of the Immaculate Conception, the other has the name of the Virgin Mary. She had them blessed, and started to distribute them. In January 1671, Pope Clement X approved the blessing and investing of this scapular.

This scapular must have a blue wool cloth, the wool must be woven. One side bears a symbolization of the mystery of the Immaculate Conception of Our Lady and on the other the name of the Blessed Virgin Mary.

The Blue Scapular is also included in the Fivefold Scapular. The Fivefold Scapular is made of five of the most popular scapulars sewn together on the top and connected to a single shared string. The Fivefold Scapular originally was a four-fold scapular (Brown, Black, Blue, and white), and is known as Redemptorist Scapular, since the Redemptorist Fathers were first granted special faculties, in perpetuity, by the Holy See to bless and invest the scapulars in 1803 and to enrol the faithful into the respective confraternities. In 1847, the Red Passion Scapular was added to the other four to become the current form of Fivefold Scapular, and in 1886 Pope Leo XIII gave permission to bless and enrol the five scapulars cumulatively, and later the Church extended the faculty (to bless and enrol the Fivefold Scapular) to any priest.

Responsibilities of Those Wearing the Blue Scapular and Belonging to the Confraternity[94]

These special graces and indulgences are granted only if people honour the Immaculate Conception of the Blessed Mother through:

- Wearing the Blue Scapular day and night;
- Living a life of chastity according to their station in life;
- Showing special devotion to the Most Holy Virgin Mary in the mystery of her Immaculate Conception;
- Praying for the conversion of sinners and for God's mercy on the whole world.

---

[94] Information regarding enrolment from: "The Blue Scapular Prayer Book to Accompany the Scapular of the Immaculate Conception" by Licheń Stary, (2021) pp.48-57.

The Confraternity of the Immaculate Conception: Its Aims and Spiritual Benefits[95]

The Congregation of Marian Fathers' Confraternity of the Immaculate Conception of the Most B.V.M. is a private association of the faithful who, living in the world and participating in the spirituality, apostolate, and mission of the Congregation of Marian Fathers, particularly spread devotion to the Immaculate Conception of the Most B.V.M. and pray for the deceased, while striving for Christian perfection in the manner proper to their station in life.

Confraternity members share (both during their lifetime and after death) in the Congregation's spiritual benefits. The Confraternity's aims are:

• *To help its members, living in the world, in their striving for Christian perfection according to the spirituality of the Congregation of Marian Fathers.*
• *To spread devotion to the Immaculate*

---

95 **NOTE:** it is possible to be invested with the Blue Scapular, without joining the Marian Fathers' Confraternity. You will not share in the full benefits of that confraternity. Instead, those invested will belong spiritually to the broadly understood community of the Theatine Fathers—custodians of the Blue Scapular. In addition, they share in the spiritual benefits of the Archconfraternity of the Immaculate Conception located at the Sant'Andrea della Valle Basilica in Rome, which is run by the Theatine Fathers. See the last point under 'Additional Explanations, other obligations and Privileges'.

Conception of the Blessed Virgin, and to assist the deceased suffering in Purgatory.

Confraternity members, vested with the Blue Scapular, shall always devoutly wear it as a visible sign in honour of the Immaculate Conception of the Most B.V.M. and a distinguishing feature of those who are particularly devoted to the Most Blessed Virgin Immaculately Conceived.

Membership in the Confraternity obliges the members to spread devotion to the Immaculate Conception of the Most Blessed Virgin by imitating her virtues, but above all by living in the state of grace.

It also obliges them to continuously dedicate a certain amount of time to meeting the Lord in prayer, to frequently participate in the Eucharistic Sacrifice, and to pray and meditate upon the Rosary.

+ Confraternity members are to recite and offer daily for the intention of the deceased the Chaplet of the Ten Evangelical Virtues of the Blessed Virgin (see Appendix Four for this chaplet), OR, the Divine Mercy Chaplet, AND the Salve Regina prayer.

They may also offer for the intentions of the Poor Souls their deeds of mercy, sufferings, and trials of life, as well as voluntary self-denial and mortification.

It is recommended for the Confraternity members to frequently invoke Mary's protection with short ardent prayers such as;

+ *"Immaculate Queen of the Holy Scapular take me under the mantle of your protection;"*

+ *"O Mary Conceived without sin, pray for us who have recourse to thee;"*

+ *"May the Virgin Mary's Immaculate Conception be our health and protection,"* and

+ *"Blessed be the holy and Immaculate Conception of the Most Holy Virgin Mary."*

As faith-filled persons involved in the life of the Church, Confraternity members shall participate in the life of their parish community and support the priests in various ways, especially in the work of evangelisation in their own parish. They should also spread the scapular devotion and encourage others to join the Confraternity of the Immaculate Conception. Confraternity members should participate in periodic meetings presided over by the local Promoter of the Confraternity, for the purpose of revitalizing their sense of belonging, learning the spirituality of the Marian Fathers, and strengthening their awareness of the needs of their neighbour, doing all of the above in close communion with Mary. They should also support the Marians with their prayers and alms; finding new friends for the Congregation and praying for good and holy Marian vocations.

Confraternity members share in all spiritual benefits of the Congregation of Marian Fathers of the Immaculate Conception of the Blessed Virgin:

- Fruits of the daily Masses celebrated by the Marian priests, and Masses for the intentions of the living and deceased associates of the Congregation of Marian Fathers.
- The right to enrol their deceased loved ones in the Memorial of the Holy Masses celebrated by the Congregation in the entire month of November and in the Solemn Vespers sung during the Octave of All Souls Day.
- Fruits of the daily prayers recited by the members of the Congregation.
- Supernatural fruits of the merits, good deeds, and indulgences obtained by members of the Congregation.

Feast Days and Indulgences

By virtue of receiving and wearing the Blue Scapular of the Immaculate Conception of the Blessed Virgin Mary and by the power of the directives of the Apostolic See of February 2, 1968, and of March 30, 2012, Confraternity members may obtain a plenary indulgence under the usual conditions on the day of receiving the Scapular and their admission into the Confraternity, as well as on the days listed below.

The primary feasts of the Confraternity are:

- The solemnity of the Immaculate Conception of the Most Blessed Virgin Mary (Dec. 8);
    Confraternity members shall live out the solemnity of the Immaculate Conception in profound

love and gratitude to God and Mary. On this day they shall renew their devout commitment to her service, their faithfulness to Christ and His Church, and shall entrust to the maternal Heart of the Immaculate Virgin the entire Marian family.

- The Commemoration of All the Faithful Departed (November 2).

On the day of All the Faithful Departed, Confraternity members shall commend to God through prayers, sacrifices, and indulgences the souls of the departed suffering in Purgatory.

Indulgences:

Those who wear the Scapular of the Immaculate Conception can receive a plenary indulgence under the usual conditions[96] on the following days:

- The day of investiture with the Scapular of the Immaculate Conception;
- The solemnity of the Immaculate Conception of the Most B.V.M. (December 8);
- The feast of Presentation of the Lord (February 2);
- The solemnity of the Assumption, (August 15);
- Christmas Day (December 25);
- Easter Sunday;
- The solemnity of the Ascension;

---

96   Usual conditions: to gain a plenary indulgence one must 1) be in the state of grace and free from all attachment to sin, even venial sin; 2) have a general intention to gain the indulgence; 3) perform the required acts to obtain the indulgence; 4) receive the Sacrament of Reconciliation and Holy Eucharist; 5) pray for the intentions of the Holy Father.

• The liturgical commemoration of St. Stanislaus Papczyński, Founder of the Marians (May 18);
• The liturgical commemoration of St. Cajetan, Founder of the Theatine Order (August 7).

❦

Order of Admission and Investiture Ceremony

Introductory Rites

When the people or simply the members of the confraternity have gathered, the celebrant enters during the singing of a hymn suited to the particular celebration. After the singing, the celebrant says:

Celebrant: In the name of the Father, and of the Son, and of the Holy Spirit.

All make the sign of the cross and reply: **Amen.**

Celebrant: Through the Son, born of Mary, every blessing comes to us from God our Father. May His grace and peace be with you all.

All reply: **And with your spirit.**

In the following words, the celebrant prepares those present for the admission and the blessing:

Celebrant: God uses ordinary things as signs to

express His extraordinary mercy toward us. Through simple things as well we express our gratitude, declare our willingness to serve God, and profess the resolve to live up to our baptismal consecration. The Blue Scapular is the sign of entrance into the Marian Fathers' Confraternity of the Immaculate Conception of the Most Blessed Virgin Mary. This scapular thus expresses our intention of sharing in the spirituality of the Congregation of Marian Fathers. That intention renews our baptismal resolve to put on Christ with the help of Mary Immaculately Conceived, whose own greatest desire is that we become more like Christ in praise of the Trinity, until, dressed for the wedding feast, we reach our home in heaven.

The Reading of the Word of God

A reader, one of those present, or the celebrant reads a text of sacred Scripture, taken either from the readings in the Lectionary for Masses in honour of Our Lady or one of the following excerpts.

(A Reader or the Celebrant): Brothers and sisters, listen to the words of the Prophet Isaiah: Is 61:9-11.

Their offspring shall be renowned among the nations, and their descendants in the midst of the peoples; all who see them shall acknowledge them: They are offspring the Lord has blessed. I will rejoice heartily in the Lord, my being exults in my God; for he has clothed me with garments of salvation, and wrapped me in a robe of justice. Like a bridegroom adorned with a diadem, as a bride adorns herself with her jewels. As the earth brings forth its shoots, and a garden makes its seeds spring up, so will the Lord God make justice spring up, and praise before

all the nations.
                    The word of God.

All reply: **Thanks be to God.**

Or this may be read:

(Reader / Celebrant): Brothers and sisters, listen to the words of the Letter of St. Paul to the Ephesians: Eph 4:17, 20-24.

So I declare and testify in the Lord that you must no longer live as the Gentiles do, in the futility of their minds; that is not how you learned Christ, assuming that you have heard of him and were taught in him, as truth is in Jesus, that you should put away the old self of your former way of life, corrupted through deceitful desires, and be renewed in the spirit of your minds, and put on the new self, created in God's way in righteousness and holiness of truth.
                    The word of God.

All reply: **Thanks be to God.**

After the reading, the celebrant gives a homily.

The Intercessions

The intercessions are then said. The celebrant introduces them and an assisting minister or the one of those present announces the intentions.

Celebrant: Relying on the intercession of the Virgin Mary Immaculately Conceived, who by the power of the Holy Spirit gave the Word our flesh, so that we might share in the grace of our firstborn brother and live for the glory of God, let us pray to the Father, saying:

All respond: **God, grant that we may put on Christ**.

Reader: Father, you willed to have your beloved Son take on our humanity, so that in Him we might share in Your own life; grant that we may be called and truly be Your children. For this we pray.

All: **God, grant that we may put on Christ.**

Reader: You wished Christ to be in every respect like us, but without sin, so that in following Him we might share in His filial image; grant that we may follow Christ so as to please You in all things. For this we pray.

All: **God, grant that we may put on Christ.**

Reader: You call those who are clothed in the wedding garment of the kingdom to the feast of Your grace, where You reveal Yourself to them; teach us to serve You loyally. For this we pray.

All: **God, grant that we may put on Christ.**

Reader: You clothe us with the robe of righteousness and holiness, so that though the Holy Spirit we may live for You. Show forth the holiness of Your Church and through Christ make us grow in holiness, so that we may work together generously for the salvation of others. For this we pray.

All: God, grant that we may put on Christ.

Reader: You continually bestow on us in Christ every spiritual blessing, until, clothed in the wedding garment, we go out to meet Christ at His coming; grant that through the prayers of Mary we may pass from death to life. For this we pray.

All: God, grant that we may put on Christ.

The Prayer of Blessing

With outstretched hands, the celebrant continues:

O God, the author and perfecter of all holiness, You call all who are reborn of water and the Holy Spirit to the fullness of the Christian life and the perfection of charity. Look with kindness on those who will join today the Confraternity of the Immaculate Conception and who will devoutly receive the Blue Scapular in honour of the Blessed Virgin Mary Immaculately Conceived. As long as they live, let them become sharers in the image of Christ Your Son and, after they have fulfilled their mission on earth with the help of Mary, the Virgin Mother, receive them into the joy of Your heavenly home. We ask this through Christ our Lord.

All: **Amen.**

Admission to the Confraternity

Those to be admitted into the Confraternity approach the altar and remain standing.

Celebrant: Our help is in the name of the Lord.
    All: Who made heaven and earth.
C. Lord, hear my prayer.
    A. And let my cry come to You.
C. The Lord be with you.
    A. And with your spirit.

C. Let us pray;
    O God, who by the Immaculate Conception of the Blessed Virgin prepared a worthy dwelling for your Son, grant, we pray, that, as you preserved her from every stain by virtue of the death of Your Son, which You foresaw, so, though her intercession, we too, may be cleansed and admitted to Your presence. Through Our Lord Jesus Christ, your Son, who lives and reigns with You in the unity of the Holy Spirit, one God for ever and ever.

    All respond; **Amen.**

Celebrant: In virtue of the power entrusted to me, I accept you into the Marian Fathers' Confraternity of the Immaculate Conception of the Most Blessed Virgin Mary. By joining this Confraternity, you accept the commitments that entitle you to share spiritually in the life, prayers, and good works of all the Marian priests and brothers, both during your lifetime and after death. In the name of the Father, and of the Son, and of the Holy Spirit.

    All: **Amen.**

The celebrant sprinkles the newly admitted with

holy water, upon which they kneel and recite after the celebrant the following <u>Act of Oblation</u>:

Most Blessed Virgin Mary, Mother of God and Immaculate Virgin, I, *(here each person mentions his/her name)*, a poor and sinful person, most unworthy to see your holy face, wish to serve you. Trusting in your great mercy, in the presence of your beloved Son, Lord Jesus, our Saviour and Master, and of all the Angels and Saints, I offer myself today into your bondage of love as the most devoted child in the Confraternity of your Immaculate Conception, taking you as my special Mother, Lady, and Protectress. I firmly resolve never to leave you and always to defend your honour. I especially promise that I shall promote the mystery of your Immaculate Conception until death. Therefore, I humbly ask you, most Blessed Virgin, through the Blood of your only Begotten Son Jesus Christ, to mercifully receive me among the ranks of your servants as your eternal slave; to help me in all my troubles and needs; and, above all, to come to my assistance at the hour of death as the Mother of Mercy. Amen.

Investiture with the Blue Scapular

The newly admitted to the Confraternity remain kneeling and the celebrant continues with the prayer of the blessing of the scapular. The following formula can be used also when the ceremony of blessing and investiture with the scapular is not combined with the admission into the Confraternity.

Celebrant: Lord Jesus Christ, You chose to share our human nature. We humbly ask You to bless this scapular made in honour of the Immaculate Conception of the Most Blessed Virgin Mary. Grant that those who are clothed in it lend themselves to moral renewal among people. And may this those, Your servant(s), invested with the scapular, through the intercession of the Virgin Mary Immaculately Conceived also deserve to be clothed in You, who live and reign for ever and ever.

All: **Amen.**

The celebrant sprinkles the scapular with holy water and places it over the shoulders of the recipient, saying:

Celebrant: Brother/Sister, receive this Blue Scapular, from now on a sign of your belonging in the Confraternity of the Immaculate Conception of the Most Blessed Virgin Mary, that by her help you may divest yourself of "the old man." May God grant that you may wear it cleansed of every sin and free of all stain, and thus pass into eternal life.

All: **Amen.**

Celebrant: By the authority delegated to me, I extend to you a share in the spiritual benefits of plenary indulgences and other graces bestowed upon those who are vested with and worthily wear the Blue Scapular. In the name of the Father, and the Son, and the Holy Spirit.

All: **Amen.**

The Concluding Rite

The celebrant, with his hands outstretched, concludes the rite with a solemn blessing. All those present bow their heads:

Celebrant: The Lord be with you.
　　All: And with your spirit.

C. Bow your head(s) and pray for God's blessing. May the Lord, who redeemed the world through His Son born of the Virgin Mary and who deigned to accept you into the Confraternity of her Immaculate Conception, grant you His blessing.
　　A. **Amen.**

C. May the Most Blessed Virgin Mary, who gave us the Giver of Life, protect you always.
　　A. **Amen.**

C. May the Lord grant health, true joy, and eternal happiness to all present here today to honour the Immaculate Virgin.
　　A. **Amen.**

Then he blesses all present:

C. And may Almighty God bless you all, the Father, ✠ and the Son, and the Holy Spirit.
　　A. **Amen.**
C. May the Virgin Mary's Immaculate Conception be your health and protection.
　　A. **Amen.**

It is recommended to end this celebration with a suitable hymn.

❀

Additional Explanations, other Obligations and Privileges

• It is necessary to go to Communion on the day of joining the Confraternity of the Immaculate Conception of the Blessed Virgin and receiving the Blue Scapular. The scapular should be made out of blue woven wool cloth. The scapular should be worn so that its one part is over the chest and the other over the back.

• In 1910, St. Pope Pius X introduced a scapular medal, which may be substituted in most cases for any of the various cloth scapulars if there is a valid reason for substitution and not for 'frvioulus' motives. However, enrolment in the scapulars must be made with a cloth scapular before the substitution.

• Both the cloth scapular and the medal should be worthily worn. When the Blue Scapular wears out or becomes misplaced or lost, another scapular should be put on; the replacement can be blessed by any priest or deacon. (Since this obligation mentions a blessing, it is apparent a replacement Blue scapular must be blessed and is not like the Brown Scapular which does not need to be blessed when replaced.)

• People wearing the Blue Scapular also share in all the spiritual benefits of the Order of the Clerics Regular Theatines, both during their lifetime and after death.

- The names of the faithful belonging to the Confraternity of the Immaculate Conception should be recorded in the registry of the Confraternity. Some of the Marian churches at which the Confraternity exists (i.e. in Warsaw-Stegny, Poland, or in London, the United Kingdom) have such a registry. In the U.S. The Confraternity is established at the National Shrine of The Divine Mercy in Stockbridge, Mass. Confraternity members receive a special certificate confirming their membership.

- The death of a Brother or Sister of the Confraternity (the honorary title of a member) should be reported to the respective Marian church, so that the Congregation can include that person in their prayers for the departed.

- The pious wearing of the scapular and devotional practices—as for example, kissing the scapular or medal—carry an additional partial indulgence granted by the Church.

- **There is the opportunity of accepting the Scapular of the Immaculate Conception of the Most Blessed Virgin Mary <u>without</u> joining the Marian Fathers' Confraternity.** <u>The faithful who wish to accept the Scapular but do not want to belong to the said Confraternity should clearly state this when asking for the Scapular.</u> The faithful who wear the Blue Scapular but are not formally aggregated (admitted into the Confraternity of the Marian Fathers and listed in their Register) **belong spiritually to the broadly understood community of the Theatine Fathers—custodians of the Blue Scapular. In addition, they share in the spiritual benefits of the Archconfraternity of the Immaculate Conception located at the Sant'Andrea della Valle Basilica in Rome, which is run by the Theatine Fathers.**

Appendix Three

The Red Scapular of the Passion

Story of the Red Scapular

Louise-Apolline-Aline Andriveau was born on 7 May 1810 in Saint-Pourçain-sur-Sioule (Allier) to Leonardo and Apolline Andriveau. Her father was a notary who ensured that she received a good education. When her father was given a promotion the family moved to Paris. After the death of her mother it was decided that she should complete her studies at the convent of St. Elizabeth.

In 1833, she joined the Daughters of Charity of Saint Vincent de Paul as Sister Apolline, and was sent to the convent in Troyes where she spent the next thirty-eight years. At first, she taught school but was later assigned to visiting the poor and caring for the chapel. She had a particular devotion to the Passion of Christ.

Then in 1846, from July 26 to September 14, she had visions of Jesus and Mary. She declared:

"I saw, or thought I saw, Our Lord dressed in a flowing robe of a red colour with a blue mantle hanging from His shoulders... Oh! Love of Jesus Christ, how You filled my heart at that moment! Oh! How beautiful He was! It was no longer the painful expression, the sorrowful face worn with suffering that I had seen in Pilate's hall a few days before during Mass. It was beauty itself! In His right Hand He held a scapular upon which was a crucifix surrounded by those instruments of the Passion which caused His Sacred Humanity to suffer most. I read around the crucifix: *'Holy Passion of Our Lord Jesus Christ, save us.'* At the other end of the red woollen braid was a picture of the Sacred Hearts of Jesus and Mary, the one surrounded with thorns, the other pierced by a lance, and both surrounded by a cross."

Sister Apolline described how she shuddered upon seeing Jesus rudely struck against the wood of the cross and quoted the Blessed Virgin Mary as saying that the "world is hurrying to its perdition because it considers not the Passion of Christ... . Do all you can to bring (to mind) and consider His sufferings. Do all you can to save the world."

According to the revelation, to wear the blood-red scapular was to be "clad in the livery" of Christ's Passion and that it would prove to us a strong armour against infernal assaults, an impenetrable buckler against the arrows of our spiritual enemies and, according to the testimony of Jesus Christ, to all who wear it with faith and piety it will be a pledge of pardon, a source of grace.

Christ revealed during the vision of September 14, the Feast of the Exaltation of the Holy Cross:

"The priests of the Mission[97] alone are to give this scapular, and those who wear it when blessed by them will receive every Friday a full remission of their sins, and a great increase of faith, hope, and charity."

Bl. Pius IX approved the use of the scapular on June 25, 1847. He further granted to the priests of the Congregation of the Mission (Vincentians) the faculty of blessing the scapular and investing the faithful with it. The Superior-General was allowed to communicate the faculty of blessing and investing the scapular to priests outside the Vincentian order and such a scapular can now be invested by any Catholic priest.

---

97   i.e. the Vincentians.

The Design of the Scapular

The Red Scapular is unique in that it and its straps or bands must be made of red wool, the material of the straps cannot be substituted with any other material, and unlike most scapulars it is adorned with specifically described images which are essential to it and cannot be altered.

One side of the scapular shows a crucifix, some of the Instruments of the Passion, and the words "Holy Passion of Our Lord Jesus Christ Save Us." The other side depicts a small cross above the Sacred Heart of Jesus and the Immaculate Heart of Mary plus the words "Sacred Hearts of Jesus and Mary, protect us."

The Red Scapular is also part of the Five Fold Scapular and is the first on top or is the 'outer' scapular so the Passion symbols may be the first seen, and also apparently, the red wool bands cannot be changed, while the four other scapulars do not have this requirement and their straps may be different to the main material.

Obligations of the Red Scapular Confraternity Members

Every member is required:

- To enrol in the Confraternity register
- To wear the Red Scapular constantly
- Each member to to regularly attend their holy duties
- To meditate or think up Our Lord's Passion and death occasionally for a few minutes. (Apparently, the daily practise of this is required.)

Indulgences Granted by Bl. Pius IX to the Red Scapular Confraternity Members[98]

~ For all those who wear the Red Scapular, shall every Friday be granted an indulgence of 7 years and 7 quarantines (280 days), if the receive Holy Communion and recite 5 Our Fathers, 5 Hail Marys and 5 Glory Be's in honour of the Sacred Passion.

~ An indulgence of 3 years and 3 quarantines (120 days) for meditation one half hour on the Passion.

~ An indulgence of 200 days for kissing the scapular with compunction while saying the prayer: *"We beseech Thee, therefore, help Thy servants, whom Thou has redeemed by Thy Precious Blood."*

~ A plenary indulgence to members who on every Friday, having gone to confession and received Communion, shall meditate devoutly for some time on Our Lord's Passion, and pray for the following intentions: for peace and concord among Christian states, for the extirpation of heresy, and for the exaltation of Holy mother Church.

---

[98] Information from "Scapular of the most sacred passion of our Lord Jesus Christ: with rules explanatory for obtaining the indulgences as granted by His present Holiness Pope Pius IX.", James Duffy, Dublin, (1848).

Investiture Ceremony[99]

The one who is to receive the scapular is kneeling. The priest, vested in surplice and red stole, says:

P: Our help is in the name of the Lord.

---

[99] I have not been able to find much information on this, other that the investiture ceremony of the Five Fold scapular. The source I found says this investiture ceremony for the Five Fold Scapular was taken from the *Rituale Romanum*, and that the ceremony for the Red Scapular was officially approved by the Congregation of Sacred Rites June 25, 1847. We can only hope the ceremony provided here is still accurate and in use. (Source: www.catholicaromana.org/uploads/8/6/4/2/86424754/scapular_investitures.pdf)

As for enrollment, I have not found much information on this either, except some parishes obviously still do it, if you can find them. At the time of this publication, I discovered one such parish in Washington State that enrols new members every First Friday during the even months at

St. Joseph Parish,
121 E. Maple St. Sequim,
WA 98382. Tel. (360) 683-6076, USA.
E-mail: sj@clallamcatholic.org,

... and during the odd months this takes place at:

Queen of Angels,
209 W. 11th St, Port Angeles,
WA 98362. Telephone (360) 452-2351.
E-mail: qa@clallamcatholic.org

If you are near these churches and interesting in enroling, you may give your details online here:

All: Who made heaven and earth.
P: The Lord be with you.
All: May He also be with you.

P. Let us pray.

Lord Jesus Christ, who condescended to clothe yourself in our mortal nature, and to despoil yourself, taking the form of a servant and becoming obedient, even to the death of the cross; we humbly beg you in your boundless goodness to bless ✠ this garment, designed as a reminder of your bitter passion and of your Sacred Heart, as well as a reminder of the loving and compassionate heart of your immaculate Mother. May this servant of yours, who is to wear it, all the better meditate on these mysteries; and may he (she), by the merits and prayers of the blessed Virgin Mary, likewise put on you. We ask this of you who live and reign forever and ever.

All: Amen.

Then the priest sprinkles the scapular with holy water, and invests the person with it, saying:

P. Take, dear brother (sister), this sacred garb, and divesting yourself of the old man, put on the new man. May you wear it with honour and thus attain everlasting life.

All: Amen.

https://clallamcatholic.org/red-scapular-investiture/

If you are having difficulty finding a place to enrol near you, considering enroling in the Five Fold scapular. Or, perhaps try encouraging your local pastors to begin the practise of this devotion in your parish as any priest may enrol new members.

Then the priest continues:

By the faculty granted me I make you a partaker of all the spiritual benefits with which this holy scapular is endowed by privilege of the Holy See; in the name of the Father, and of the Son, ✠ and of the Holy Spirit.

All: Amen.

In conclusion the following versicle is said three times:

We therefore implore you to save your servants whom Your Precious Blood redeemed. Amen.

Appendix Four

The Chaplet of the Ten Evangelical Virtues of the Blessed Virgin Mary

The Marians have recited this prayer since the time of approval of the Order upon the "Rule of the Ten Evangelical Virtues of the B.V.M." by Pope Innocent XII in 1699. Saint Stanislaus Papczynski, Founder of the Marians, was the first to make his solemn vows on this rule in Warsaw, on June 6, 1701.

To pray the Chaplet, which consists of one decade, use only 10 beads of a Rosary or a 10-bead chaplet.

* Begin with the Sign of the Cross

* Say one Our Father

* Say the ten Hail Marys, but each time vary them as follows:

Hail Mary, full of grace, the Lord is with thee, blessed art thou among women, and blessed is the Fruit of thy womb, Jesus.

Holy Mary, Mother of God, *(here add each of the ten virtues into the prayer):*

1: **Most pure,** pray for us sinners now, and at the hour of our death. Amen.

2: **Most prudent**, pray for us sinners now, and at the hour of our death. Amen. (Etc., each time).

3: **Most humble,**

4: **Most faithful**,

5: **Most devout,**

6: **Most obedient,**

7: **Most poor,**

8: **Most patient,**

9: **Most merciful,**

10: **Most sorrowful,** pray for us sinners now, and at the hour of our death. Amen.

Conclude the decade of Hail Marys with:

V. **Glory be to the Father and to the Son and to the Holy Spirit:**

R. **As it was in the beginning, is now and will be forever. Amen.**

V. **In Your Conception, O Virgin Mary, You were Immaculate.**

R. **Pray for us to the Father Whose Son, Jesus, you brought forth into the world.**

Let us pray:

Father, You prepared the Virgin Mary to be the worthy mother of Your Son. You let her share beforehand in the salvation Christ would bring by His death, and kept her sinless from the first moment of her conception. Help us by her prayers to live in Your presence without sin. We ask this in the name of Jesus the Lord. Amen.

V. **The Virgin Mary's Immaculate Conception,**
R. **Be our Health and our Protection.**

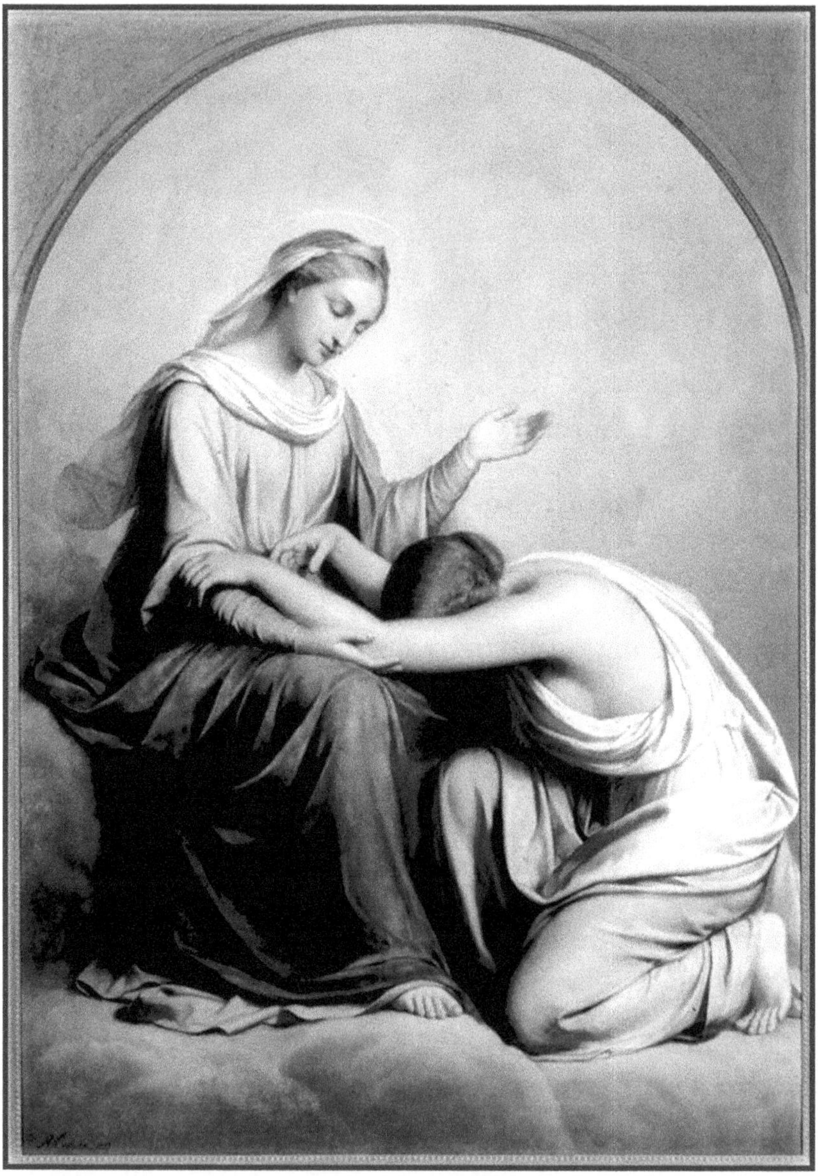

Hail, Holy Queen,
Mother of Mercy,
Hail, our life, our sweetness, and our hope!
To thee do we cry,
poor banished children of Eve,
To thee, do we send up our sighs,
mourning and weeping
in this valley of tears.
Turn them, most gracious advocate,
thine eyes of mercy towards us,
and after this, our exile,
show unto us
the blessed fruit of thy womb,
Jesus.

O clement, O loving, O sweet Virgin Mary!

V. Pray for us, O holy Mother of God,
 R. That we may be made worthy
of the promises of Christ. Amen.

Illustration Credits[100]

Page 26: "*Virgin Mary and Child*", Julius Hübner (1806-1882). Artvee, public domain listing.

Page 31: "*View of Chartres Cathedral*", (Origin: Paris. Date: 1700 – 1799). Rijksmuseum, Public Domain Dedication (CC0 1.0).

Page 32: Replica of the ancient statue of Chartres (Photo by Velsen). Image from *La cathédrale de Chartres* by René Merlet, (1900).

Page 33: Chapel of Our Lady Sous Terre, (Photo by Neurdein). Image from *La cathédrale de Chartres* by René Merlet, (1900).

Page 34: "*The Assumption of the Virgin*" (c. 1500), Michel Sittow (Flemish, 1468 – 1525). Artvee, public domain listing.

Page 39: The Veil of the Virgin at Chartes. Photocredit - "Photograph by Rama, Wikimedia Commons, Cc-by-sa-2.0-fr" (Changes: photo originally in colour; changed to black and white for black and white text publication.)

Page 41: Chartres Cathedral, Chartres, France (1922) by Paul B. Travis. Artvee, public domain listing.

Page 42: "The Immaculate Conception", Padre Manuel 'El Jesuita'. Artvee public domain listing.

Page 46: *Chartres Cathedral*, Giuseppe Canella (1788 – 1847). Artvee, public domain listing.

Page 49: "*The Virgin of the Immaculate Conception with Saints Catherine of Alexandria, Augustine of Hippo, Nicholas of Bari, Nicholas of Tolentino and Gregory the Great*", by Maratta. Artvee, public domain listing.

---

100 - Creative Commons images were originally in colour – they have been changed to black and white for this publication. Any other changes if and when made are listed with the particular images.

Page 52: "*Beleg en vergelijk van Chartres*", (Siege of Chartres) 1568, etching by Frans Hogenberg, after Jean Perrissin, 1565 – 1573. Rijksmuseum, Public Domain Dedication (CC0 1.0).

Page 54: "*Saint Mary (the Blessed Virgin) with the Christ Child, Saint Jerome and Saint Francis of Assisi and angels.*" Engraving by G. Asioli after F. Rosaspina after L. Carracci. Wellcome Collection, public domain.

Page 59: "*Saint Mary (the Blessed Virgin) with the Christ Child.*" Engraving by J.L. Appold after L. Veneziano. Wellcome Collection, public domain.

Page 62: *Carmel convent a Rue d'enfer 1860s*, by Léon Leymonnerye, (1803 - 1879), Musée Carnavalet, Histoire de Paris. Paris Musées Collection, public domain.

Page 65: *Notre Dame 1860s*, Edouard Baldus (French (born Prussia), 1813–1889). Albumen silver print from glass negative. Metropolitain Museum of Art. Public domain listing.

Page 67: "*Immaculate conception*", (from 1685 until 1688), Carlo Maratti (Italian, 1625-1713). Artvee, public domain listing.

Page 71: "*Saint Mary (the Blessed Virgin) with the Christ Child*", engraving by J.L. Appold after L. Veneziano. Wellcome Collection, public domain listing.

Page 73: "*Duns Scotus*", attributed to Federico Zuccaro, Italian, 1540/41-1609. Date: c. 1560. Art Institute of Chicago. Public domain listing.

Page 74: "Louis XIV in Notre-Dame de Paris on January 30, 1687 at a Thanksgiving Service after his Recovery from a Grave Illness", by Guy Louis Vernansal the Elder (ca. 1710–15). Metropolitan Museum of Art. Public domain listing.

Page 76: "*The Virgin of the Rosary with Saint Catherine of Alexandria and Saint Catherine of Sienna*", (1611). Luis Lagarto. Artvee, public domain listing.

Page 83: "*The coronation of the Virgin in Heaven*", etching by C. Schut. Wellcome Collection, public domain.

Page 89: "*The Creation of the World and the Garden of Eden*", (1560). Anonymous. Artvee, public domain listing.

Page 97: "*The Virgin of the Immaculate Heart*", engraving. Wellcome Collection, public domain.

Page 98: Front and reverse of the Miraculous Medal. Illustrations from "*The Miraculous Medal: Its Origin, History, Circulation, Results,*" by M. Aladel, C.M., (1880).

Page 99: Vision of Our Lady appearing to St. Catherine with the Medal and rays of grace. Illustration from "*The Miraculous Medal: Its Origin, History, Circulation, Results,*" by M. Aladel, C.M., (1880).

Page 101: "*Noah's ark on the Mount Ararat*", Simon de Myle (Dutch, 16th century). Artvee, public domain listing.

Page 106: "*Notre Dame de la Garde I, Marseilles, France.*" Date between ca 1890 and ca 1900. Photochrom print, creator unknown. Library of Congress. Public domain.

Page 113: "*Benoîte Rencurel*" (Apparition at Laus), by AntonyB - CC BY-SA 3.0 l . Openverse site.

Page 114: "*The Infant Moses*", (c. 1876-c. 1878), by Gustave Moreau. Artvee, public domain listing.

Page 119: 2005-09-17 10-01 Provence 547 , "*Avignon - Kathedrale Notre-Dame-de-Doms*", by Allie Caulfield. Openverse site. CC BY 2.0 license.

Page 122: *"Moses Before the Burning Bush"*, (1663) by Claude Mellan. Metropolitan Museum of Art. Public domain.

Page 124: *"Penne-d'Agenais - Basilique Notre-Dame de Peyragude"* by Jacques MOSSOT is. Openverse listing licensed under CC BY-SA 4.0

Page 128: (Moses striking the Rock) Decorations from the Villa Pelucca (Part IV: Left Wall: Story of Moses). Bernardino Luini, (1475?-1533?). Frick Digital Collection, public domain.

Page 131: (The fever stone),La pierre des fièvres. Cathédrale du Puy-en-Velay. Haute-Loire. Photograph by 'Espirat', May 23, 2011. CC BY-SA 4.0. Wikimedia Commons.

Page 133: (Black Virgin of Puy statue.) "Cathédrale Notre-Dame-de-l'Annonciation du Puy-en-Velay", photograph by Konrad Hädener, licensed under CC BY 2.0. Openverse listing.

Page 136: *"Joshua passing the River Jordan with the Ark of the Covenant"*, (1800), by Benjamin West (1738-1820). Artvee, public domain listing.

Page 140: (Notre Dame de Grâce), *"Cambrai cathedrale ext.jpg"*, by 'Velvet'. Openverse listing, licensed under CC BY-SA 4.0.

Page 146: *"File:Basilique Notre-Dame d'Avesnières 17.JPG"*, photograph by Romain Bréget. Openverse listing licensed under CC BY-SA 3.0.

Page 151: *"Moses On Mount Sinai"*, by Jean-Léon Gérôme (1824-1904). Artvee, public domain listing.

Page 161: (Crypt chapel, Trinity Church, Ronceray), - *"Angers - Église de la Trinité - Crypte – 20080921.jpg"*, by Sémhur Openverse listing, licensed under CC BY-SA 4.0.

Page 167: *"The Ark Passes Over the Jordan"*, (c. 1896-1902) by James Tissot (French, 1836-1902). Artvee, public domain listing.

Page 171: "*Joshua and the Israelites before the Walls of Jericho,*" (c. 1600), by Christoph Murer, (1558–1614). National Gallery of Art, Washington, [No Copyright – United States (NoC US 1.0)]. Listing from Look and Learn Site.

Page 174: (Altar of Notre Dame des Ardilliers), "*File:Saumur (49) Église Notre-Dame-des-Ardilliers - Intérieur 04.jpg*" by "GO69". Openverse listing licensed under CC BY-SA 4.0.

Page 176: "*Ark of the Covenant in the temple of Dagon*", etching by Caspar Luyken, print maker, Noord-Nederlands (1672–1708). Rijksmuseum, Public Domain Dedication (CC0 1.0).

Page 183: (St. Ours Church, Loches), '*Stadt Loches im Département Indre-et-Loire*', (October 25, 2008) photograph by Gerd Eichmann. Wikimedia Commons, CC BY-SA 4.0.

Page 187: "*Sanctuaire Notre-Dame-du-Marillais, Le Marillais, Mauges-sur-Loire*", (July 28, 2018). Photograph by "GO69". Wikimedia Commons, CC BY-SA 4.0.

Page 190: "*La statue de Notre-Dame-du-Chef-du-Pont, dans l'église Saint-Thomas de La Flèche*", (July 27, 2012). Photograph by "HubertduMaine". Wikimedia Commons, CC BY-SA 3.0 (Note-changes to this photo: original photo has been cropped for this publication.)

Page 193: "*The Immaculate Conception*", Guido Reni. (1627). Metropolitan Museum of Art. Public Domain.

Page 198: "*The Coronation of the Virgin*", (ca 1492). Sandro Botticelli. Artvee, public domain listing.

Page 205: "*St. Simon Stock Receiving the Brown Scapular*", cover image from: "The novena in honor of Our Lady of Mt. Carmel : followed by a notice of the origin, privileges, and blessings of the brown scapular." (1931).

Page 248: "Les litanies de la Vierge", (1857) by Auguste Legras, (1817-1887). Artvee, public domain listing.

If you liked this book
you may also like these by
Fr. Marin de Boylesve:

**A Thought for
Each Day of the Year**

ISBN: 978-9893319956

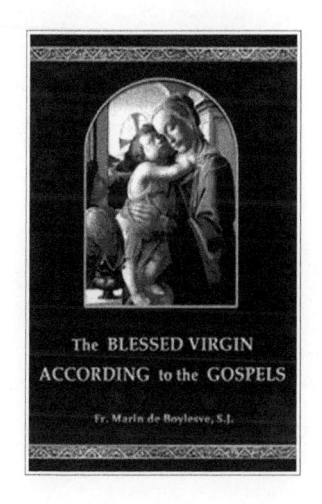

**The Blessed Virgin
According to the Gospels**

ISBN: 978-9895372607

**Little Month
of Saint Joseph**

ISBN: 978-9899684485

The First and Second Joseph

ISBN: 978-989-53726-2-1

The Sacred Heart of Jesus

ISBN: 978-9893328071

The Month of the Precious Blood

ISBN: 978-9893328088

The Month of Saint Michael

ISBN: 978-9899684492

The Month of Saint Teresa

ISBN: 978-9895372614

Other books by E.A. Bucchianeri by Subject

Prophetic Visions:

* We Are Warned: The Prophecies of Marie-Julie Jahenny (E-book)

- Marie-Julie of the Crucifix: Stigmatist and Prophet (E-book)

The Faustian Legend:

* Faust: My Soul be Damned for the World, 2 Vols.

Lord of the Rings:

* Lord of the Rings: Apocalyptic Prophecies (E-Book)

Classical Music:

* Handel's Path to Covent Garden

* A Compendium of Essays:
Purcell, Hogarth and Handel, Beethoven, Liszt, Debussy and Andrew Lloyd Webber

Fiction Novels:

* Brushstrokes of a Gadfly

* Vocation of a Gadfly

Phantom of the Opera:

* Phantom Phantasia: Poetry for the Phantom of the Opera Phan